1145

Hope you enjoy,

[illegible]

CIVIL WAR TALES

by
Gary C. Walker

Cover art by:
Patsy Arrington Dorset Rortraits
234 West Augusta Ave.
Vinton, Va. 24179
703-342-8367

Proof reading by:
Nancy Francisco
2728 Colonial Ave. SW # 11
Roanoke, Va. 24015

ISBN 0-9617898-9-7

Second Edition
Printed for:
A & W Enterprise
P. O. Box 8133
Roanoke, Va. 24014

This book is
proudly dedicated to
the mother of the bride
Mildred Ratcliffe Adams

Thank you, beautiful wife and bride, Sue A. Walker, for the many hours you spent preparing the manuscript.

Table of Contents

INTRODUCTION

Story telling is as old as mankind. Many Biblical experts believe that parts of the Bible are stories that are told and retold, maybe through several generations, before being recorded in print.

I have chosen to record some stories related to the Civil War (or War Between the States if you prefer) for several reasons. The foremost of these is that the stories were not being repeated. These precious accounts are being lost from our society, and America's culture is diminished with each loss. I have recorded some tales so that they will not perish.

The main reason the family tales are not being retold is the advent of mass public communication. With the general public's acceptance of radio, people became listeners to a voice with no body. When television followed, social intercourse fell to a very low level. When families gather, they don't talk; they turn on the tube and stare.

This has had a profound effect on our entire society. The older people were once revered as storehouses of knowledge and wisdom and as the keepers of family history. Now they are called elderly and viewed increasingly as burdens, not blessings. Their worth to their families and society has been greatly reduced.

Not only have older people been affected; we all have lost. There is less family pride. One last name is as good as another when there is no history behind that name, when there are no tales of past glories and accomplishments.

When I was young, I was admonished: "Never do anything that would tarnish the family name, because the family name is important and stands for honorable behavior."

Perhaps part of the root cause of juvenile delinquency can be traced to the loss of family history. If the name stands for nothing, there is nothing for the child to uphold. One more link that held society together is going and, in some cases, completely gone.

I suffer no delusion that this book will reverse recent history, that families will turn off the radio and television and talk of family history, that this will reverse traditional values and cure all ills of society. But maybe the reader will stop to think of what is being lost and will do his part to try and prevent it from happening.

Most of this book is based on oral information, although much is supplemented by written accounts. Research was done in an attempt to verify and clarify some facts. In most of the stories, the original storyteller is dead. The stories have been told and retold, and some inaccuracies have naturally occurred. Some facts related to the stories are beyond my ability to research for accuracy. Because the war has never truly ended, some of the stories do have modern settings with their roots anchored in the war.

As I researched this book, I interviewed numerous people; and I was amazed at the findings. First, we hear so much about the mobility of American society I was struck by the fact that the majority of the people I interviewed lived within one-hundred miles of the place where their

ancestors lived between 1861-65. Admittedly, this may be a very biased section of the population. Perhaps those who love their historical roots are not as mobile as society in general. Because I collected stories of those who live relatively close, this book contains somewhat more stories about Southern ancestors than Northern ones.
There was no scheme to write this book with a pro-Southern slant. I was attempting to collect interesting tales and to present them with as little author bias as possible. All of the stories have the war as their base; some have more modern settings because this was a war that never truly ended.

The second thing that shocked me was the very brief accounts that remain in some cases. The war of 1861 was America's largest, most devastating conflict; but all that some people can recall of their ancestors and their involvement can be easily summarized in four sentences. It almost brings tears to my eyes to know that only four sentences remain from those who lived, fought, and died during those times.

I used the language or expressions of the times or of the storyteller in an attempt to communicate the mood of the times or of the storyteller. Approximately sixty percent of the battles during the war occurred in Virginia. At least, that percent of the stories in my book also took place in Virginia; therefore, if a location is not followed by a state name: it is Virginia.

I would like to thank each person who gave so freely of his time as I researched this book, and that includes the stories that were given to me but were not chosen for publication.

People gave me information, both oral and written, supplied me with photographs or allowed me to take photographs, and I credited the source of the information at the end of each story (in most cases). I combined their material with my research and knowledge of history to create the story. Sometimes the information they gave me had to be changed to conform with proven fact.

Sometimes the slant of the story was changed in order to make the story more interesting. I hope the people who granted me the interview will be pleased. I hope none will be offended.

In several stories the participant(s) or the source are not named. There are reasons for this. Some stories are about deserters or wrongdoers, and the source of the information requested that the last names be deleted in order not to embarrass some people today because of the deeds of their ancestors. Some people gave me information on family histories that were not their own family's. Because some of the information was negative, they requested that no family names be given. Some people so highly cherish their privacy that they do not wish their names given. Still others said they would welcome others who shared a common interest, so both their names and addresses were included. Some people have relics or keepsakes that they value greatly, and they did not wish to have their names in print. Most stories are simply followed by the source's name, and no address is given. If you wish to communicate with one of these persons, simply send a letter to that person in care of A&W Enterprise, P.O. Box 8133, Roanoke, Va. 24014, and I will forward the unopened letter to that person.

In some cases, the story is followed by more than one name. This is my way of saying thanks to those who helped me with their expert knowledge. Without such help, some stories could not be told.

I hope that the pages that follow will bring both great joy and great sadness to the reader. I hope that you will be entertained; but, most of all, I hope that by the end of the book you will have a greater understanding and appreciation for our history.

As with my other books, I have greatly enjoyed writing this for you. As with my other books, I hope this book too will light another candle in the darkness to help everyone to understand and better appreciate the deeds of our forebearers.

No Story

I had decided to open this book much differently. I had decided to go on page after page about the need for this book; the need to preserve war history and family lore. But then I met Garnett S. Miller, Sr. and Garnett S. Miller,Jr. When Garnett, Sr. informed me that he had a Civil War drum in his family, my ears perked up. "Tell me about it," I said.

"It was passed down through the family. We don't know where it came from. It is supposed to be Union. That's all we know." was the reply.

The drum is in reasonably good shape. Some of the cord is loose, and there is a hole in the bottom. Where did it come from? Was one of the Miller clan in the Union Army? Did he beat cadence and commands for boys in blue? Did a Miller in gray capture the war trophy in battle?

UNION DRUMMER BOY

Art Work By: Robert R. Wagner
1 West Milford St.
Mount Union, Pa. 17066

Was it a Miller who returned from the war with the drum, or was it someone in a related family line? Could someone other than a Miller or relative have been the one to return from the war with the drum and it became a possession of the Millers by gift, barter, or luck? The drum cannot speak, and the questions cannot be answered.

If the drum could speak, it might tell of the beat of early morning reveille in one of the thousands of recruitment camps throughout the North. It could tell of the cheering crowds that lined the roads to say "goodby" to their sons who now wore a Union uniform.

It could speak of long, tiring marches, of the tension in the air when it beat assembly for battle. It could speak of its drummer(s) and their commanding officer(s). It could speak of beaten commands that rent the air when shells split the sky, the ground shook, and the air burned. It could speak of glory, honor, cowardice, and dishonor, of victory and humiliating defeat. It could speak of conquest and capture. Oh, the stories that old drum could tell if it could only speak.

The tap of the drum is like a dirge played throughout the Miller family. Something very important is dead. The loss is incalculable. The older family members who knew of the drum's story failed to speak of it to the younger members. All is lost.

"A picture is worth a thousand words," but there are so few to go with this one.

The Miller family has lost, and so have we all. No matter what our last name, we could all be like this Miller family. Because of time and economic restraints, only a relatively few of the countless Civil War stories can be preserved between the covers of this book. I am glad to do that, but it is incumbent upon each of us to preserve our family history. If you can't write, tell the stories over and often to your family members, especially to the young. If you can't write, at least set the essential facts down on a sheet of paper.

The poet asks:
"Will there come a time
When the memories fade,
And pass on with the long, long
Years?
When the tie no longer binds?
(Then the poet prayed)
Lord, save me from this darkest fear."*

Unfortunately, the answer is yes. The time has come in the Miller family. Let the readers of this book resolve that no dirges will echo through their family. Lord, save us from this darkest fear.

Courtesy: Garnett S. Miller, Sr.
Garnett S. Miller, Jr.

*From musical: "Stonewall Country"

RESURRECTION OF THE DEAD

Lt. C.H. Spangler, 28th Regiment Virginia Infantry, was captured by the Union Army. Along with a group of Confederate prisoners, he was force marched north all day, with the ultimate destination being a Union prison. As they marched, Spangler formulated an escape plan.

As the sun was sinking low, the prisoners were given a rest break. Spangler told his comrades, "Boys, I would rather be buried alive than go to a Northern prison; and if you boys will dig me a grave and bury me, when it gets darker and you move on, I will come out and make my escape."

The prisoners agreed to his plan, and Spangler played dead. It is unclear as to what was

CAPTURED CONFEDERATE SOLDIERS

supposed to have caused the death of Spangler, but the other prisoners played their roles well. Undoubtedly, Union guards gathered about the body of Spangler and saw no signs of life. They probably didn't examine the body closely because whatever killed this Reb might be catching. It is probable that they kicked the body and when Spangler didn't react, the commander ordered the other prisoners to dig his grave quickly. The plan was working.

A shallow grave was rapidly dug and Spangler's body placed in it. Quickly, the prisoners threw dirt and brush on Spangler so the Yanks would not notice his breathing. A prayer was said for the departed, but not dead, lieutenant. Then two empty wooden hardtack (a form of hard bread) boxes were stacked as a head stone for Spangler.

Art Work by: Diane Hindenlang 3755 New Spring Branch Dr. S. E. Roanoke, Va. 24014

Spangler was just one more dead Reb and one less problem for the guards. With some daylight left, the prison column continued north.

The plan was working well. All Spangler had to do was let time pass, and darkness would conceal his escape. The grave was dug too short, and Spangler was in a cramped position; but that was okay because he didn't intend to use the grave on a permanent basis.

About dark, the peace of his gravesite was disturbed by men walking and talking." More Yanks?" thought Spangler.

Indeed, it was another Union unit; and they decided to make camp for the night close to his gravesite. Spangler knew he was going to have to be dead longer than he had anticipated. Now he wished that his buddies had dug the grave a little longer. The confinement was causing muscle cramps and spasms. As pain increases the rate of time decreases. Minutes seemed like hours to Spangler. Being dead was much harder than he had expected.

The Yankees neither knew of nor cared about the problems of a dead man. They started making camp. As darkness and the Union troops settled in, the amount of activity in the camp decreased; and Spangler could hear no noise. Were there Yanks sitting on his gravesite, or had they gone? Spangler wondered.

At least one Yank, a recent immigrant from what is now Germany, was still cooking his supper. He spied the empty hardtack boxes and decided to steal the monument to a dead Reb and use it to cook his supper.

As the Yankee soldier approached the grave, the pain of cramped muscles forced Spangler to decide to leave his grave. At the same moment that Spangler shook the dirt off of his head, the Union soldier was reaching for the crate. Spangler listened for a moment and said to himself, "I believe they have gone."

The sight of this Rebel coming out of his grave talking scared the wits out of the Yankee soldier. He let out a yell and ran towards camp hollering in his thick German accent, "Mien Gott! The Rebel! The Rebel! He raise from the dead! I leaves this country right away quick: I no stay where dead Rebel raises from dead again! No good to kill him!"

The German's cry attracted attention to himself and Lieutenant Spangler. Other Union soldiers investigated this miracle and decided that this Reb was not Jesus Christ the second but that he was a Union prisoner for the second time.

This time, his march north to a Union prison was not interrupted by deception or a miracle.

Lieutenant Spangler did survive the war, and it was many years before the need was felt to bury him again. Because he had experienced an uncomfortable grave once, it is said that Spangler's final wish was that he be measured and a roomy, comfortable grave be dug for him. His relatives, former comrades in arms, and friends carried out his last request and wished him a comfortable rest until he is resurrected for the second time.

Courtesy: Roy Hayth

WHEN JOHNNY COMES MARCHING HOME AGAIN

The Confederacy was no more. There were shouts of jubilation, bands playing, and prayers of thanksgiving in the North. There was deep depression and weeping in the South. "When Johnny Comes Marching Home Again" was to be sung with glee throughout a victorious Confederacy, but there was no singing, no joy, when and if Johnny came home again.

The word from Appomattox spread like a pall over the area. The Paul family had received the

Art Work By: Travis Clark
Box 1631
Honaker, Va. 24260

news at their plantation of Otterbein west of Dayton. In gloom, the family contemplated what was lost, the cost, and what may lie ahead. They wondered constantly about their Johnny, "John Paul." The last they heard, he was alive; but that was almost two months ago. Was he still alive or did he lay corpse in the trenches of Petersburg, or Richmond, or somewhere over the road to surrender? Had he been felled by a Yankee bullet and now lay in an unmarked grave? Would his fate and final resting place remain unknown to his loved ones?

The gloom that gripped the South and held Otterbein in its sway was lifted a little several days after the surrender, for their Johnny did come home again. Yes, he was as skinny as a fence rail, but all the soldiers were. Yes, he was dirty and bone weary, but he was alive and home. But he arrived in a way the family never thought of. After four years of war, death, pain, and misery, there were no tears left that their Johnny could shed for his beloved Confederacy, his lost youth, and his comrades. In an attempt to show his emotions for the Cause that was now lost, John Paul had ridden his horse facing backwards all the way from Appomattox to Otterbein.

Courtesy: John Grey Paul

THE EMPTY SWING

Large families and the natural processes of life generate their own entertainment. Lenna was the last of thirteen children in the Wright family. She was born shortly before the war but was too young to fully appreciate the destruction and terror that gripped Washngton County during her early years.

She may not have fully understood the Cause for which her kinsmen had struggled and died, but she knew there was a reverence that ran deep in the family for the departed Confederacy.

Being the youngest child allowed Lenna more time to play while the older children did their chores. She enjoyed sneaking about and watching her older brothers and sisters as they did the chores, taunting them because she didn't have to

Art Work by: Robert R. Wagner 1 West Milford St. Mount Union, Pa. 17066

work.

The visit of any stranger always caught Lenna's interest. If she could be close, she was in the middle of the visit; but if it were a time for adults only, Lenna was still as near as possible, spying on the guests.

When a potential beau came to call on her older sister, Nancy, Lenna was told in no uncertain terms to stay away. She heard the words, but her curiosity was more than she could control.

The young beau was greeted in the front parlor by the family; and, after a brief time, Nancy and the boy were left alone. As the rest of the family left the room, Lenna was also forced to leave. With the parlor door shut, Lenna could not pursue her favorite pastime of snooping.

After what seemed like an eternity, the young girl heard the front door open and close. Through a window, she saw sister Nancy and the boy walk around the house.

The house had a room attached to the back, thus forming an "L" shape. This "L" shape would provide cover for the snooping Lenna.

Young Lenna crept as quietly as a mouse along the wall until she could peek around the corner of the house. There she saw her sister being pushed gently in the swing, only yards away. She was close enough that she could hear their voices clearly.

The beau and Nancy were making general conversation as they were getting to know each other. They swang and talked for some time.

The beau said, "I was with the army in Buffalo during the war."

The Southern girl, Nancy, wanted to make sure that her ears were not deceiving her. "Buffalo, New York?" she asked.

"Yes," was his reply.

With that, Nancy dug her heels into the dirt, stopping the swing abruptly. "Our army was never in Buffalo! Good day, Sir!" retorted Nancy. Without one word more, she left the swing and the damn Yankee standing and went inside.

The jilted beau stood holding the ropes, looking first at the empty seat and then at the sight of Nancy walking away. After some time, he left, still in shock and confusion.

Courtesy: M. Flemming Ring.Jr.

YOUNG REBEL

Thomas N. Hutson recalled that he grew up on Main Street in Salem. The guns of the War Between the States were long silent, but the glories and Southern pride remained.

A neighbor, Mrs. Rose Roberts, President of the local United Daughters of the Confederacy, was still fighting her father's war over seventy years later. She was so Southern that she refused to carry Lincoln pennies in her purse. Her influence on the neighbor boy, Thomas, was great; and soon he and his young friends re-enacted Pickett's charge over and over in the fields near town.

In the 1940's, the guns of war rumbled again. Thomas, only age sixteen, standing five feet, seven inches, and weighing less than one-hundred pounds soaking wet, answered the call. He was given a machine gun and assigned to the 2nd Marine Division, 6th Regiment, Company A, 1st Battalion. He was delighted to learn that he was not the youngest or smallest in his outfit.

During an interview, he said something about "the Yankees." The article about him in **The Leatherneck Magazine** was titled "Young Rebel." The nickname stuck, though shortened to "Reb," during his service time.

His former neighbor was so proud of the "Young Rebel" that she mailed a small Confederate battle flag to him in New Zealand. Thomas proudly carried the flag in his shirt pocket through many battles and campaigns.

On Saipan, Thomas's unit was hit hard by a Japanese tank attack. In the confusion of night battle, lines merged; and it was unclear where the enemy's tanks were and where the United States' tanks were. From his position, Thomas could clearly tell that it was a Japanese tank closing in on him! He fixed a grenade in the launcher on his rifle and let it fly! Scratch one enemy tank. In the dark, Thomas saw another tank in the distance but assumed it to be American.

His assumption was wrong. The tank's cannon roared. "It's true you never hear the one that gets you," said Thomas. In fact, he didn't feel it either. It was only when he reached for his rifle with his right hand that he realized something was wrong. The fire from the burning tank provided light enough to see that his right hand was dangling from his arm.

"I'm hit!" he yelled. His lieutenant, an old man of twenty-six, said, "Where?" Thomas held up his hand to the light. The lieutenant gave an expression of his revulsion.

The attack was so great that the position and Thomas had to be abandoned. There along a dirt road, Thomas was having trouble breathing; and blood was gushing with every beat of his heart. Not only was his arm severed, but also a piece of shrapnel had pierced the flag and his chest wall, severing an artery and puncturing one lung. Thomas plugged the hole with his thumb.

Despite the pain and blood loss, Thomas remained conscious. In the dark, he could hear Japanese troops talking as they closed in on his position. Thomas knew his only hope of avoiding death or capture if he were discovered by the enemy was to pretend that he was already dead. To aid in the deception, he used his only good hand and repeatedly dipped blood from his chest wound and smeared it on his face. The blood dried, and he was not discovered.

Through the eternity of that night, Thomas saw the flashes of light and heard the sounds of

Thomas N. Hutson

battle. At daybreak, the promise of his buddies came true; and they returned for him. He was taken to an aid station. His wounds were bandaged. Only after a nurse washed away some of the dried blood did she exclaim, "I didn't know you were a white man."

He was taken to a hospital ship off shore, but the Japs started to shell that ship also. Thomas remarked, "I began to think they were after me personally."

While lying on a stretcher, Thomas became aware that an orderly was taking the tape off his dog tags. Thomas and some others in the outfit had taped them so they would not rattle and give their positions away. "Why?" asked Thomas. "I want to see what religion you are," replied the orderly. "Am I bad?" asked Thomas. "Very bad," was the reply. "Get them all," said Thomas (meaning Catholic, Protestant, and Jew). He wanted to cover all the bases. Soon a Catholic priest administered the last rites, but it was premature.

Thomas was taken into surgery where the gangrenous hand was removed. Also, his uniform was cut from his body. Thomas tried to speak but could barely whisper. He tried to gesture with his feeble hand, but nothing worked. The uniform with the pierced Confederate flag, now soaked in blood, was taken away.

This brave man mourns the loss of the flag almost as much as the loss of his hand, nearly fifty years later.

Courtesy: Thomas N. Hutson

Recreation:
Union artillery pounds Confederate position

DAMN LUCKY

John Padgett may have been very brave or very foolish, but all agree that he was damned lucky. When battle raged hot and minie ball and shell filled the air, soldiers hugged the ground behind their breastworks and prayed hard for deliverance. Most soldiers, that is. In the thickest of battles, it was not uncommon to see John "climb out from behind the breastworks and present himself as a target to be shot at."

Almost a half a million men met their Maker during those four years, but John Padgett marched home "without a scratch."

Courtesy: Rudy Padgett

PRIVATE FARLEY CHANGED THE WAR

When historians gather and talk about the war, they talk about the brilliant strategy of Lee, the tenacity of Grant, the daring of Forrest, and the steadfastness of Sherman. They talk of the great battles of Manassas, Shiloh, Gettysburg, and Vicksburg. But they never talk of Private Wesley Farley and the minor rear-guard action that changed the course of the war.

History couldn't have picked a less likely hero than Wesley Farley. He was born in Virginia in 1838. His home was nestled among the crags of what is now Logan County, West Virginia. Wesley had a limited education and worked a rocky, dirt-poor farm in the mountains.

When war came, the vast majority of the mountain boys elected to join the forces of their native state. Logan Wildcats was their name, and they felt like young tigers when they mustered into Confederate service as Company G, 22nd Virginia Infantry Regiment.

Most of his neighbors joined the 22nd, but Wesley's heart was not in their cause. He became a member of Company I, 7th West Virginia Cavalry. The Logan area became bitterly divided before war's end. It was one of the few places in the nation where old men or young boys could elect to join a home guard unit that was either Northern or Southern.

The man who would be Wesley's claim to fame was also a Virginian, born ten years before Wesley. He too was a farmer, a cavalryman, and his outfit was also number seven; but that is where the similarities stopped. The worlds of Farley and the man he would kill were far apart.

Turner Ashby was the son of Virginia aristocracy, born on the family plantation of "Rose Bank" in the heart of the rich, flat land of Fauquier County. Young Turner's family supplied him with a series of private tutors, so he became well educated.

When John Brown raided Harper's Ferry, Turner raised his own company of men to put down the revolt. Although too late to assist Colonel Robert E. Lee, Turner's initiative and personal leadership were noted.

At war's start, Turner's men became part of the 7th Virginia Cavalry. In a few months, Captain Ashby was saluted as Gen. Turner Ashby by his men. He was known for his "daring and brilliance" in Jackson's Valley Campaign. The mighty "Stonewall" appointed Ashby to the command of his entire cavalry division.

If it had not been for war, the widely separate worlds of Wesley and Turner would never have collided, and the number seven would have never fought the number seven. The paths of the private and the general would never have crossed.

Early in the war, Jackson had pulled off one more amazing strategy and was moving off the battlefield with the infantry. Ashby moved the cavalry to cover the rear of Jackson's army. Ashby was directing minor, inconsequential action a few miles from Harrisonburg.

Wesley and other members of the 7th (Union) saw a Southern officer on a white horse at some distance. Several guns, from the 7th roared;including Wesley's, horse and rider went down. The distance was too great to see the rank or assess any wound that may have been inflicted to the officer.It was the next day before the 7th learned that enemy General Turner Ashby was dead!

Recreation:
Federals firing on Confederate position

Once the death of the famous general was announced, there were a slew of pretenders to Private Wesley Farley's claim to fame as "The man who killed Turner Ashby." Men from other companies of the 7th West Virginia said they had slain the great general. Captain Curtis, Company E, said, "I did it." "No," said Sergeant Smar, "I did it." Colonel of the regiment, Cluseret, puffed himself up and said, "I did it." Wesley argued with that bunch of lying jerks until he was red in the face.

"Judging from the time that I fired until the rider was struck, no other bullet but mine could have possibly struck the general," or words to that effect (sometimes interspersed with profanity) was what Wesley said.

The 7th was divided and almost ready to make war on each other when that bunch of uppity Pennsylvania boys came grinning by. The boys from Pennsylvania called themselves "Bucktails" and looked down their snooty noses at the country bumpkins from the mountains. "Nothing as great as shooting the enemy general, Turner Ashby, could have been done by the 7th," they declared. In fact, it was a member of their company who shot Ashby.

"A damn lie," roared Wesley. The Pennsylvania boys were out of ammunition and had left the field to get replenished when Ashby was shot.

A monument was erected to Gen. Turner Ashby on the spot where he fell. Historians speculate "what if" Ashby had lived to continue to lead Jackson's cavalry, "Would the war have turned out differently?" Many people know that Ashby is buried in the Stonewall Cemetery in Winchester.

No one ever says "what if" Wesley Farley had not been near Harrisonburg in June 1862. There is no monument to him. Few people know where in Logan County he is buried.

Courtesy: W. Darrel Miller

I AIN"T GOING TO TEXAS

Peter Cooper was a poorly educated farm boy when he joined Company K, 12th Indiana Cavalry Regiment. Peter was luckier than most soldiers. He drew easy duty. He helped guard Washington City from a fort near Carrolton, Maryland. The food was good; he drilled twice a day, made more money than he had in his whole life time, and had Sunday off. The farm boy was having the time of his life. "I have more fun in one day here than a whole week back home," he said.

While comrades in blue were dying by the thousands, lucky Peter was sent to guard a captured railroad in Alabama. About twenty-five men in his company took a Southern family's home to use as their living quarters. With army rations and what they could take from the community, they lived well. They built a breastworks of brick, but the closest to action Peter came was when he spotted Rebels two miles away.

Next, Peter pulled an even better assignment: guard duty in New Orleans. Peter sent money home and spoke of love and marriage to a neighbor girl when he returned. While fellow soldiers slopped through muddy trenches and dodged bullets in Virginia, Peter was surrounded by green grass, "Peach trees ... in full bloom and the oranges gang thick (in) the trees." War is hell!

Peter pulled short stays of duty in Louisville and Nashville and was in Memphis at war's end.

In April 1865, Peter was looking forward to his release from the army. His suffering in comfort, and his close call with combat was over, he thought. The rumor spread like wild fire in the regiment. The cruel war was not to be over for them; they had done such a good job guarding away from combat the War Department was sending them to Texas to guard as occupation troops. "Damn," thought Peter. "The army has gone too far this time." He told fellow soldiers: if the rumor is true, "I, for one, am going to desert ... If they get this child to Texas, they will have to play sharper than I can."

Lucky Peter did not desert, or go to Texas, or go home. He was struck down by the most deadly enemy the soldiers on both sides faced during the war: disease. A letter home from one of his comrades said: "... Hard to tell you that your son died ... He had a good coffin so I guess he is as well off as if he had a golden coffin."

Courtesy: Diane Canary

LET THE GAME-STOP

In the late stages of the war, Southern defenses were crumbling everywhere. Union columns entered the old South almost at will .One such column drove deep into Southern territory and found itself on the north bank of New River, approximately two miles east of Austinville.

On the south bank of the river stood "the Shot Tower." The tower was built of massive stones and mortar. It was several feet thick at the base and extended approximately one-hundred-feet into the air. There were no other man-made structures close by, so it projected greatly on the high bluff south of the river. The tower had been built in colonial days to produce shot for shot guns. Molten lead was dropped from the top. As the lead fell, it hardened into round pellets. (During the war, most bullets were molded; therefore, the Shot Tower had no military value.)

Regardless of its military importance, it made a tempting target for the Union column on the north bank. There were two cannon with the Federals. Because there was no Confederate opposition, the Union gunners decided to make sport of hitting the Shot Tower. The men unlimbered both guns, took aim, fired, and missed. Which crew would hit the target first? The mounted troops cheered their favorite gun crew on.

The report of the guns brought a senior officer to the scene. When he realized that it was a game they were playing and not accomplishing anything of military value, he called a halt to the firing and ordered the men not to... destroy the tower,"Southern folk will need rabbit shot when the war is over."

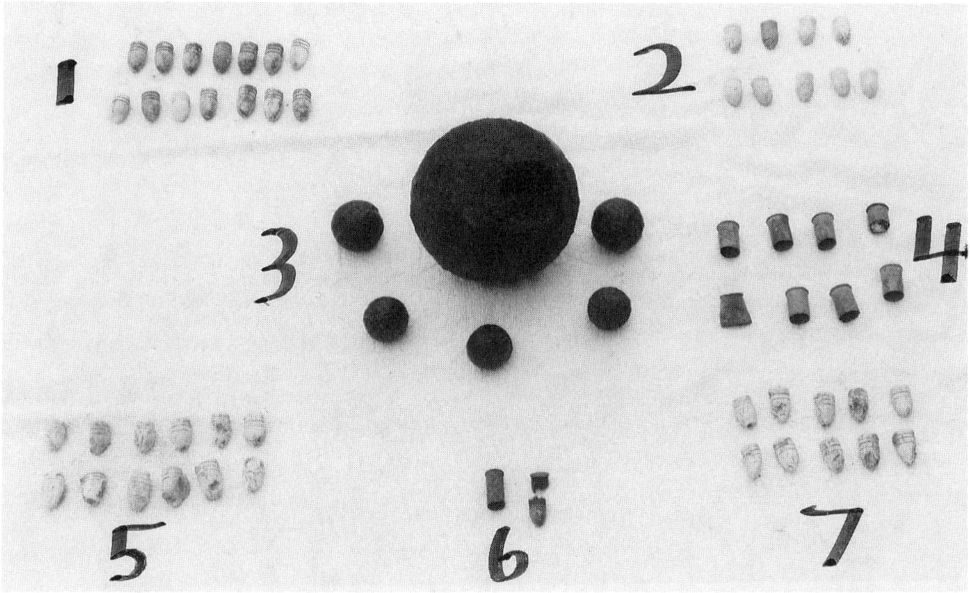

Most projectiles used during the war were molded. These are examples of molded projectiles. 1- 58 Cl. minie balls 2- 52 Cal. Star Carbine 3- 12 pound cannon ball surrounded by grape shot 4- 52 Cal. Spencer Repeating Rifle cartridges 5- 58 Cal. minie balls 6- 44 Ca. Ballard Carbine 7- Spencer

Courtesy: Pat Trout Collection

The Union officer's action stopped the contest and helped preserve history. If the game had continued, there would be no Shot Tower State Park today; nor would the image of the tower be proudly displayed on the great seal of Wythe County.

Courtesy: M. Flemming Ring, Jr.

SHOT TOWER-WYTHE COUNTY

Disobeying The Mighty Stonewall

It was raining; the wind was blowing, and Gen. James A. Walker had just bedded his boys down for the night when a courier came into camp with a dispatch. General Walker read the order. It was from the commander of the army, "Stonewall" himself.

General Walker felt the order made damned little sense. He was directed to have his men strike their tents, pack their gear, get soaking wet, march a few hundred yards into a soggy field, and set-up camp again.

"Stonewall" was a man to be followed, not to be questioned. But without clear military reason to move, Walker decided his men's comfort was more important than following the order; so he ordered no move.

The morning broke clear, and Walker received

an order to report to a regular staff conference with "Stonewall" at headquarters. As Walker and his aide rode toward the conference, the subject of the disobeyed order came up. Walker knew he would have hell to pay for even a slight infraction of "Stonewall's" rules, so he dismounted and rolled in the mud. When Walker showed up for the conference, he grumbled about ridiculous orders to move camp in the middle of the night in a rain storm.

"Stonewall" never found out about Walker's deceit.

Courtesy: M. Caldwell Butler

A CUP OF TEA FROM THE PAST TO THE PRESENT

The Robert R. Sharkey family of Jackson, Mississippi, were very proud of their silver service. It had been bought from Tiffany's & Company, the world-famous jewelry and silversmiths of New York. It bore pattern number one and was probably bought in 1852 or 1853.

At gay parties in the summer nights, guests had refreshed themselves with tea from the service. The splendor of the antebellum South, the music, the laughter, the chivalry, and the beauty of the tea set went together.

In too few years, fire, death, dirt, and destruction had replaced all that was known. Robert was concerned about the rumors that General Sherman's army was closing in on Jackson, Mississippi. Robert was alarmed when Southern soldiers began fortifying his yard. He knew his family must flee from Sherman and the battle to come. He knew he must take what he could because there would not be much left of his property when the two armies were through using it.

Decisions had to be made as to what to take and what to leave. The silver service would stay.

The kitchen was away from the main house, and Robert felt it might not be burned even if the house were. To hide the silver service, bricks were removed from the kitchen floor, the silver service buried, and the bricks replaced.

After what could be loaded was loaded, after what could be hidden was hidden, the family fled Jackson.

Sherman had his way, and most of Jackson was burned. After he left, the Sharkey family returned to a burned out home and a burned-out kitchen. The once wealthy family was ruined. The family dug through the ruins to salvage what they could. After removing the debris from what was the kitchen, the family was delighted to discover the heat of the fire had not gone below the bricks. Their beautiful silver service was unharmed. In their sorrow, they rejoiced.

Though hard times were faced by them in the 1860's and thereafter, they were determined that this relic of a happier, more genteel time would not leave their possession. It never did and has been passed to generation after generation of their family to keep, love, use, but not sell, and to pass to the next generation.

Recreation:
Union cavalry plundering

At least once a year, the old silver service is gotten out and cleaned. Descendants of Robert Sharkey fill their cups and remember the good times and bad and their priceless link to the past.

Anonymous

I'M NO BIRD

By the 1930's, Mr. Barnette was a frail old man with a long, white beard. When the weather was pleasant, he often strolled to the local filling station-garage in Salem, to congregate and socialize with other men from the neighborhood.

Sometimes he would stroke his beard, lift his face heavenward, and let his mind recall the days of his youth when he was Private James Barnette and wore a Confederate uniform.

One experience he recounted for the group was not forgotten. Gettysburg, Pennsylvania, was a long ways from the home of his youth. The sun beat down, and the temperature went up as the armies prepared for the third day's engagement (July 1863) in the largest battle to ever occur in the Western Hemisphere. His regiment stepped from the treeline and formed in the open field. As he looked to the left and right, there were men and flags as far as the eye could see.

recreation:
Confederates awaiting orders to attack

He could see the enemy's position in the far distance. There were a few contours in the land but no trees to speak of between the regiments, aligned for battle, and the enemy on a slight rise.

The cannon roared, and the men stood in the sunshine, just waiting. After what seemed like hours, the line began to move at a slow walk. The flags flapped in the breeze.

When the regiments came into the range of the Union's cannon, the pace quickened. He could see the smoke and fire belch forth from their cannon. Shells exploded overhead and on the ground. Southern boys fell in crumpled agony.

The Southern pace became quicker until they were in full charge. The pace of incoming Union projectiles and minie balls also quickened. The sounds of men and guns were deafening. Men fell left and right, like wheat before the Grim Reaper's scythe. The attack pressed on.

Young Barnette saw his regiment's flag fall and its bearer cut down. A comrade picked the precious banner up and advanced. The depleted regiment, screaming and yelling, followed the flag into the smoke of hell.

A second time the flag fell, but another soldier in the regiment grabbed it and held it aloft again. Murderous canister fire tore big holes in the ranks as the attack pressed on.

When standing in the field, Barnette was in the rear of the regiment; now close to the Union line, he was in the front. Barnette saw the flag fall for the third time. He was close. The flag must be borne forward, so he picked it up and led the charge.

Now close to the lines, he saw only smoke and Yanks to the left, Yanks to the right, and Yanks straight ahead. With a quick glance over his shoulder he realized that his regiment was no more. He was virtually by himself.

For his regiment and himself, the battle was over. He then said he turned about and "ran as fast as I could back toward the tree line."

Art work by: Price Youngman
Oak Hollow Arts
Box 4428
Martinsville, Va. 24115

One of the locals at the garage asked defiantly, "Why did you run from the damn Yankees?"

In a flash Barnette fired back, "Because I couldn't fly, you damn fool."

Courtesy: Thomas H. Hutson

STRETCHING THE TRUTH

Green C. Evans had a real talent for stretching the truth. After the war started, he left his home in the Carvin's Cove section of Roanoke County and stood before the doubtfilled recruiting officer.

It must have taken this lad of less than fourteen some time and many vows before he convinced the officer that he only looked young but was a full eighteen years old.

He was accepted into Company A, 14th Virginia Cavalry, but some doubt lingered because the closest he had come to the horse cavalry was driving a supply wagon for the unit.

The 14th was assigned to the Confederate Military Department of Southwest Virginia. It is not known what event(s) brought the attention of the Departmental Commander, Gen. Samuel Jones, to the Green Evans case. Jones determined that after serving the Cause for almost a year and a half, Green was still too young to serve. Jones discharged Green.

A search of the official records does not show any additional service for Green Evans after April 1863.

Many years after the war, when veterans would meet and swap stories, Green had his story too; but it wasn't a dull tale about driving a supply wagon. When others would recall battlefield glories and brave deeds, Green would reply that was okay; but "I was the personal cook for Robert E. Lee."

Courtesy: Dave Robbins

I WATCHED BOOTH RIDE BY

The war almost started forty years before the firing on Fort Sumter. The political balance of power between slave-holding and non-slave-holding

Art work by: Robert R. Wagner
1 West Milford St.
Mount Union, Pa. 17066

states was being upset. The country teetered on the brink of war, but cooler heads prevailed this time. It was decided to extend the Mason-Dixon line across the country; and those states south of the line could join the Union as slave-holding states and those north as non-slave-holding.

The year was 1820, and the settlement was known as the Missouri Compromise. Ten years later Fritz Hain was born near the small town of Red Bud, Missouri.

His family name denoted his German ancestry, but Cherokee Indian blood also coursed through his veins. He tilled the soil as he grew to manhood. When fully grown, he stood only 5 feet 4 inches tall and often wished that he were a much taller man.

The Compromise that had temporarily healed the country had done little to ease the pro- and anti-slavery factions in Missouri. When the Union split in 1861, Missourians took up arms to kill fellow Missourians. The state and families were terribly divided. Those who attempted to remain neutral, were suspected and harassed by both sides. Soon almost everyone had chosen sides to hate each other.

Fritz chose his side,the Union, and joined Company F of Dallmeyer's 6 month battalion. After six months, the war was not over; and Fritz did not return home until it was.

He knew something of the hell of fire that was Shiloh, and the muck and mire of the seige of Vicksburg. Men always gain and lose when they come face to face with possible death in combat. Fritz lost his vain wish for height at Vicksburg when a Rebel bullet parted his hair, leaving a scarlet line to mark its passing. Fritz now knew that if his wish for height had come true, his face and he would no longer exist.

During the campaigns, Fritz was the victim of discrimination. The cavalry dandies always felt they were better and smarter than the dumb infantry plodding along on the ground. The two divisions of the army played tricks and yelled taunts that often erupted into fistfights among the soldiers. Fritz developed a healthy dislike and distrust for the mounted soldiers.

Frederick "Fritz" August Hain

Some time after Vicksburg, Fritz pulled some of the best duty a Union soldier could hope for. He was assigned to the defenses of Washington City. Gone were the mud trenches, the long marches, and wet bedrolls. He now had regular hours, a clean bed, and lots of food. When not on duty, the big bustling city offered the farm boy from Missouri a wonderland in which to play.

Art work by: Travis Clark
Box 1631
Honaker, Va. 24260

On the night of April 4, 1865, Fritz was doing normal guard duty on a bridge over the Potomac. There was the normal flow of traffic, nothing unusual. The only thing that caught Fritz's attention, and then for only a minute, was when he sighted two men holding a drunk on his horse as they crossed over the bridge toward Virginia.

It was after the drunk and before midnight that some cavalry boys came dashing onto the bridge. They told Fritz that "President Lincoln had been shot." Fritz just laughed at them, thinking that the dandies were playing another joke on the infantry, trying to get a false rumor started.

It was somewhat later that Fritz was convinced by another source that Lincoln was indeed shot and that the assassin had been wounded but escaped over the bridge he had guarded out of Washington City. Fritz now realized that the drunk he had laughed at was the murderer of his Commander-in-Chief and that he had just let the assassin, John Wilkes Booth, ride by.

Courtesy: James & Maureen Worth

Bernice Rose Kettener

A GOOD YEAR

As we look back through misty, rose-colored memories, we see the old antebellum South as a romantic, idealistic society, so good that it simply could not exist. We see every man as a gentleman of honor and every woman as an elegant lady of purity dressed in a fine, flowing dress of white. Every person from aristocrat to slave was sure of his identity, station, and role in life. It was an era where religion was pervasive and sin was minuscule and universally condemned: a world of happiness, with an optimistic outlook to the future.

Virginia Smith's world must have looked bright when she graduated in the first class from Hollins Institute (founded in 1855). It was a finishing school for the fine, young ladies of the South. Many had their mammies or personal slaves to accompany them at school. Virginia always took pride in her participation as a violinist in the school orchestra.

Virginia may have met the learned gentlemen John Dexter Ribble while at college. John and Virginia married and moved to John's home in the Bradshaw area of Roanoke County. John owned land both in the Bradshaw area and on top of Catawba Mountain which looks down on Bradshaw. Virginia learned much about running the farms and about supervising the slaves because John was constantly away at the University of Virginia at Charlottesville, helping Professor Muary with his geography book. When **Maury's Geography of the United States** was published, John was very upset because he didn't receive any credit for his work, not even a minor footnote. During this period, the slaves looked to "Miss Ginny" for guidance.

The Ribble home was in Bradshaw where the rich valley lands provided good crops. The high mountain land with but a few inches of top soil was not good for intense cultivation, but grape vines grew well there. With a grape vineyard came a grape press, and a small winery was built by the Ribbles on the mountain top.

The antebellum era could not have been better to John and Virginia, the well-educated gentry of Bradshaw. They had money in the bank and crops in the field. They may have also had a finger in the silver mine at nearby Mason's Cove (where Mason's Creek flows). This legendary mine produced enough silver to make many dollars for the owners. Some say the mine was only a legend and never existed in reality. ("Charcoal" Willie Smith, a descendent of Virginia's father, believed that it did exist and spent many years of his maturity in a vain attempt to locate it.)

The constant of natural and human history is change. The Civil War became a fire-breathing dragon turned loose on the South. It destroyed and burned all that was serene and beautiful in the antebellum South, until all that was left were misty, rose-colored memories. The hot breath of the dragon was introduced to the Ribbles by Union General David Hunter's forces.

In June 1864, General Hunter's forces were in a

headlong retreat from Lynchburg; Confederate General Jubal "Old Jube" Early pursued. Because of a complicated series of maneuvers in Roanoke County, Hunter found himself engaged with Gen. John Imboden's cavalry south of Salem. Thinking that General Early was about to gobble him up, Hunter ordered cavalry division leader Gen. Alford Napoleon Duffie to open the road north at "all cost." He was to stop for nothing, and sacrifice the whole command if necessary, to open the road so that the Union wagon train and artillery that followed could escape to West Virginia.

The dust flew from the road as several thousand cavalrymen bore north out of Salem with orders to stop for nothing. A couple of miles from Salem, Union forces cut through Hanging Rock Gap along Mason's Creek. The Ribbles swore until their deaths that some of the Union soldiers found the same sinkhole that legend said was discovered by Davey Crockett. Although there is no proof that either Ribble was present, (In fact, accounts tend to show that Virginia was at the house in Bradshaw.) they both said that the sinkhole swallowed several men and horses whole.

If Duffie did lose some men and horses to an unfriendly sinkhole, this did not stop his northward dash up the side of Catawba Mountain toward the Ribbles' vineyard.

Of course, civilian outriders had spread the word to be prepared for the possibility that the Union Army was coming. Most people hid valuables, and many people ran. Some of the slaves made preparations, also. When Mr. Lincoln's horse soldiers came, many of them left (their masters). Virginia saw one of her slave girls riding on the back of one of her finest horses. Virginia ran out and stood in the path of rider and horse. The slave girl was polite when she saw Mrs. Ribble, "Hi, Miss Ginny," she said. Virginia demanded that she stop and dismount. The slave girl did neither but veered around her mistress and toward the Union Army. The last Virginia saw of the slave was her back; the last she saw of the fine horse was

Gen. Alford Napoleon Duffie

Recreation:
Union Cavalry

its rump.

Slaves leaving their masters were of no concern to General Duffie at this time because his orders were to fly north and stop for nothing. But about one-half the way up Catawba Mountain, he did stop. He was stopped by trees that had been felled across the road. (These were cut by the home guard but not by the Salem home guard as was popularly believed. The home guard unit that did the cutting was from the Catawba Iron Furnace located at Cloverdale.) The cavalry stopped, so the wagon train and artillery that followed also had to stop. The column snaked from the side of Catawba Mountain down through Hanging Rock Gap and back toward Salem.

It was an early hour of the morning, and Union cavalrymen worked hard to clear the road. By about nine a.m., the cavalry had cleared the road to the top of the mountain. Duffie sent word to the wagon train and artillery to get ready to move.

As the cavalry boys got to the top of the mountain, they saw a large white flag at some distance away and went to investigate. The Ribbles said that if their caretaker hadn't surrendered in such a big way (he actually hung a bed sheet out) that the Yankee cavalry wouldn't have discovered the winery.

The word "wine" had the same appeal to these young Federal bucks as the Siren call had on ancient mariners. It would appear that it was going to take every lad in Duffie's cavalry division to secure this one small, surrendered building. All the Yankee boys became connoisseurs of fine wine. Each wanted to sip the Ribbles' vintage and make their comments as to bouquet and flavor.

It was about this time that word arrived of the disaster occurring to the wagon train and artillery that had been stalled in Hanging Rock Gap. Confederate General John McCausland had struck the column hard. Union forces in the Gap pleaded with Duffie for cavalry protection from the Confederate onslaught. Out of a division of over 5,000 troopers, Duffie could only send a couple of companies (about 200 men). Perhaps, the rest of his command were in a holiday mood and carried away with sampling the Ribbles' wine.

It is said that the General ordered the wine kegs broken open, but the building itself was not destroyed. Maybe the Union soldiers enjoyed the bouquet and flavor so much, they didn't want to discourage the Ribbles from making their nectar in the future.

Courtesy: Virginia Ribble Parker

COAL BOMB

Most accounts of the war deal with battles in the heat of the sun; little is recorded about spying and sabotage.

The advent of the war saw an increase in the use of steam engines. Steam engines were powered by wood or coal. The Confederate saboteurs saw a way to throw a big clinker in the firebox of Union warships. They molded a cast iron shell to resemble a lump of coal. The shell was then filled with gun powder and sealed. It was not hard for a Confederate saboteur to drop one more lump into a pile of coal to be loaded onto a Union ship. The fireman would not notice anything different as he shoveled the fake coal into the firebox. The heat would detonate the gun powder and explode the firebox, spreading fire throughout the engine room. How many Union vessels were sunk by a coal bomb?

Courtesy: M. Flemming Ring, Jr.

WHO's WHO

James M. Lowery kissed his wife and family and then left his Winston County, Mississippi, home. James didn't have to go to war. Because he was a family man and a farmer, he wouldn't be drafted at this early stage of the war. Despite his exemption, James let his duty to his state and nation outweigh his home obligations.

James had several long talks with his eldest son, Joseph. Joseph, then about fifteen or sixteen, would be the man of the house. James pointed out his duties to the household and to his mother. The care of the family would be in Joseph's hands while his father took to the battlefield. There were tears and many prayers said as James left because he might die of a Yankee bullet and never come home again.

Amidst prayer and tears, James took his place in Company I, 15th Mississippi Infantry and marched off to war and possible death.

Young Joseph did his best to take care of his Mother, brothers, and sisters. Perhaps because of his age and all that goes with being a teenager, he did not unload his gun before cleaning.

It was not unusual for the family at home to receive a letter stating that their loved one had been killed in the war. One can only imagine James's thoughts as he scanned the letter telling him that his wife, mother of his children, was shot dead.

James had signed up for the duration of the war; and the army was reluctant to let him go home, even if his family might starve. Finally, an agreement was made; and Joseph entered the 15th Mississippi as a substitute for his father. James's name was never taken off the roll, and Joseph received his father's pay during the war.

Joseph was luckier than many. He returned to

his native Mississippi and married after the war. He often spoke to his wife Hannah Clark Lowery of the hardships of the war. He said that at times he was so hungry he stole hard corn from the horses to eat. At other times, the water in rain-soaked fields was so deep, men made great piles of brush to sleep on to keep out of the water. For Joseph and Hannah, the most important thing was that the war was over and life went on for them.

After the war, the Federal Government decided to pay a pension to those who served (the Union that is). This, of course, was paid from tax money collected from all parts of the country-north, south, east, and west. Those who served in the Confederate Army would receive nothing.

All states in what was the Confederacy enacted laws to provide some pension to the soldiers who served from their states. It appears that James was dead and buried before he could collect one cent of the Mississippi state pension. Apparently, no death certificate was recorded. (A recent search by a family member did not discover the final resting place of James.)

Things started getting complicated when Joseph wanted to get his pension. Because he had served the war in his father's name, the paper trail evidently was too shaky.

James left no widow because his wife had been shot accidently by Joseph. Because Joseph had served, but not in name, Joseph and Hannah felt they deserved some of the pension money for the veterans; so Hannah showed up to receive a pension as the wife of James. (James served a short time-for all the credit. Her husband served a long time-for none of the credit.)

Either the state of Mississippi didn't discover the fraud or winked at this technical breaking of the law. Either way, Hannah and James (really the son Joseph) collected the pension from the state.

Things were rolling along fine until Joseph died. Hannah had to report that her husband was deceased; but, according to the pension records, her husband was James. So even though it was

Joseph who served and died, the record showed that James had died.(This was the second time for him, and Joseph still didn't get the credit even now for dying.)

As a last honor to the veteran, the state of Mississippi erected a tombstone over Joseph's grave, stating very clearly that there lay the remains of James M. Lowery of Company I, 15th Mississippi Infantry.

It is said that often Hannah Clark Lowery could be seen placing flowers at the Rural Hill Methodist Cemetery. After all, she was the widow of James and the wife of Joseph; and she liked to visit her father-in-law's grave where her husband was buried.

Courtesy: Terry Lowery

MARKED

She was barely eleven years old when the war started. Mary L. Brown was a shy girl living a very protected life in Liberty, (now Bedford City). Talk of war frightened her: men dying with horrible gapping wounds, with smoke, death, and blood all about. She may have imagined the Yankees to be devils with long pointed tails, out to inflict pain on the good men of the Confederacy.

She had heard the rumors of Union troop's sacking, burning, and looting; but she had never seen any such behavior until the wicked Union General David "Black Dave" Hunter took control of Liberty in 1864.

Before Hunter even arrived, the whole town was in a panic. Valuables were hidden, and the roads were jammed with citizens fleeing in any direction from town except north to the Union Army. Those who couldn't run, or wouldn't run, stayed and braced for the worst. Mary and her mother stayed and endured the worst.

Like an angry swarm of blue hornets, the Union Army of 25,000 men enveloped the town. The railroad depot was burned and rails were ripped from the bed. Mills and warehouses were burned; even a hospital was burned. To the terrified girl, it seemed the whole town may burn. Union soldiers broke into homes and looted at will. Often they abused the helpless women and children. Mary did not escape this terror either.

Recreation:
Massive Union encampment

There were the crash of musketry and the screeching of shell, as men fought street to street, house to house, and hand to hand. Finally, Union forces were pushed from town.

Even with Union forces gone, the trauma was not over. Rumor was rampant that Union soldiers had poisoned all the wells. Everyone repeated the stories as if they were gospel fact about Union atrocities. Many stories related to contamination of the water supply. Union soldiers had dumped animal carcasses, manure, and other unclean things into the wells to make people become sick and die.

The only hope for the citizens was to boil the water and hope and pray that whatever was in it would not harm them. For how long a period should the citizens boil the water to drink? How long does it take to purify a well containing the carcass of a dead cat, dog, or cow? A week? A month? No one knew, but to be certain it was a long, long time.

For the traumatized girl, it took longer than most. From 1864 until her death in the 1930's, Mary Brown never drank water that had not been boiled.

Courtesy: Chris Gladden

DEAD RACE

War means death. Young men far away from their homes died from sickness and wounds. Sometimes they were not with their units and died with only strangers present. Many times in the confusion of battlefield, transport, and hospital, the soldiers passed into eternity; and no one knew their names or addresses. Often they were buried in mass graves with no markers.

It was already dark, too dark for a burial, when one such hapless Rebel passed away. He was not known in the town of Salem.

In those days, it was customary for family or friends to constantly stay with the body until the time of interment. This Rebel had neither, so a slave was assigned to stay with the corpse until morning.There was no casket for the poor dead Reb. The body was placed on a plank supported by the backs of two chairs.

The slave stayed at his station until rigormortis caused the Rebel to come to a sitting position on the boards, his eyes at least partially opened.

The slave didn't wait to see what the dead Reb would do next. He ran like a streak of lightning and didn't stop until he had put over a mile between the corpse and him.

Courtesy: Thomas N. Hutson

A PRIVATE HELL

Henry Richard Benton was born on Independence Day 1839; but when he was a man, he picked up a gun and tried to destroy the meaning of that day. He came from the Stuart Draft area.

Henry saw plenty of action and too much of death and pain. When the war was over and tales were told, he said almost nothing of the combat he had known. That was one area that was private: one area that he did not wish to recall. Perhaps it was an area he couldn't deal with and retain his sanity.

He shared very little, and his remembrances

contained no humor but centered on pain and privation. He recalled little food, bad weather, separation from loved ones, and much fatigue. The winter was icy cold, with deep snow and biting wind. When it thawed, everything turned to mud; then it froze again, and the ground became a field of swords. Small mounds of snow, ice, and mud heaved their sharp points upward. The pain to frozen feet with no shoes was incredible. Feet bled, and the pain pushed men to the breaking point. Men tied rags, straps of leather, and pieces of wood to their feet to provide some protection. Henry recalled that the best "shoes" he could come up with were pieces of burlap feed bags bound to his feet. Without good clothing, without shoes, but with hunger and pain, Henry and the army hobbled into battle.

The nearest he came to talking about combat was to recall that during the late war even the cannon had to do without. There was no more shot or shell to ram down the barrel and fire at the enemy, so the trace chains from horse's harnesses were used. Of course, once the chains were blasted through the air, there was no way to move the cannon.

To hear Henry tell it, hunger and cold were worse enemies than the Yanks. "We got some chickens," but there were no pots or pans in which to cook them. Chickens with the entrails, feathers, head, and all were rolled in the thick red mud and then cooked under the ashes and coals for a long time. When the baked clay was pulled off, it pulled off feathers and skin with it. It made Henry's children and grandchildren cringe to think of men with red clay on their hands, gnawing at the chicken carcasses; but that and handfuls of food (some stolen from the horses) kept Henry and the others alive through the war.

When Henry would recount the stories, so full of pain, when the army struggled past hope, past reason, almost past endurance but refused to say a word about the actual combat, it made the family wonder what indescribable hell lay within his memory. Until he died in 1915, he kept that his private hell and allowed no one inside, maybe not even himself.

Courtesy: Nina Varner

LEFT TO DIE ON A MOUNTAIN

When Gen. Thomas Lafayette Rosser and his cavalry were moving through Beverly, (W) Virginia, they stopped on the Ring family farm. They must have spent the night there because they left "picket stakes" behind. Picket stakes were iron rods with rounded tops. They were driven into the ground, and the horses were tied to them to prevent the horses from wandering off. Apparently, the Southern cavalry left Swope Depot (near Staunton,) and the Ring farm, headed toward Goshen Station, Warm Springs, McDowell, and then due north to Beverly. The trip was well over one hundred miles and miserable all the way. If it weren't raining, it was snowing. The streams were out of their banks, and men and animals were buffeted by the cruel weather of January 1865.

Rosser pushed his men through the night and arrived at Beverly in the predawn darkness. He placed his seven hundred men in line of battle and advanced.

Major General Thomas Rosser

By the time the Union picket sounded the alarm, it was too late: Southern soldiers quickly overpowered the Union guards. Both sides lost a few killed and wounded. The Confederates burst through the doors of the small cabins the Federals had built to protect themselves from the elements. Surprised Yanks surrendered half clothed, with no shoes and some still in their beds.

Rosser's brilliant plan to ride into enemy territory in the dead of winter and to attack before dawn was a great success. Most of the 8th Ohio Cavalry and the 34th Ohio Infantry were now Southern prisoners.

Rosser moved his column of prisoners south but was opposed every step of the way by "General Bad Weather." Men and animals broke down. Fording streams left men caked with ice and their feet frozen in boots. Men and animals could move no farther. There wasn't enough food, blankets, or clothing. The mountains along the Virginia-West Virginia border were sparsely populated. There were no large towns that the command could fall back on for shelter and food.

Rosser hadn't taken the prisoners with the intent to kill them, but it became evident that the column was only creeping through the mountains. Unless they moved more quickly, all would die of exposure: a cruel decision was made. To the victor go the spoils. Southern boys gathered the horses, best blankets, and what food they could find and rode off the mountain. The vanquished were left with very little, and the weather was intense.

The Southern cavalrymen never heard the absolute fate of the Yankees they had abandoned on the mountain, but most believed the entire lot of the poor devils died of exposure.

Courtesy: M. Flemming Ring, Jr.

THE YANKEES IS COMING! THE YANKEES IS COMING!!

Time had robbed her of her youth, but her eyes twinkled as she would tell Mollie's story, as only she could.

Mollie had no last name; she was the property of Sparrel Simmens. Mollie was young during the war. She and her mother were house slaves. Mollie had few chores to do, and she had the run of the house.

Mollie viewed her owner as a kindly, father figure. Like her mother, she referred to her master as "Captain." To her, Captain was a large man with a great bushy, black beard.

Mollie had heard the adults talk about the war and the "horrible Yankees." In her young mind, she had decided a Yankee was something like a "Bogieman."

Mollie often stationed herself on the porch and waited for Captain's return. She would then rush to open the gate for him. He always praised her for the deed and often gave her a "whole penny for her very own."

Captain left the house one day as usual; but, unknown to Mollie, he visited the barber shop. There he had his hair cut off and his beard shaved completely off.

On the porch, Mollie looked into the evening sun and saw the figure of a man approaching. She assumed it was Captain and raced to open the gate. She had never seen Captain without a beard. The terrified slave girl slammed the gate shut in her master's face and ran screaming toward the house, "The Yankees is coming; the Yankees is coming!"

When the startled inmates of the house discovered the truth, a good laugh was had by all.

At war's end, Mollie and her mother were released from slavery. Once free, Mollie and her mother needed to have a last name. With Captain's permission and to honor the household in which they had served for so many years, they adopted the name Simmens.

By the 1930's, Mollie's hair was white, but her eyes twinkled as she told of her encounter with the Yankees.

Courtesy: Thomas N. Hutson

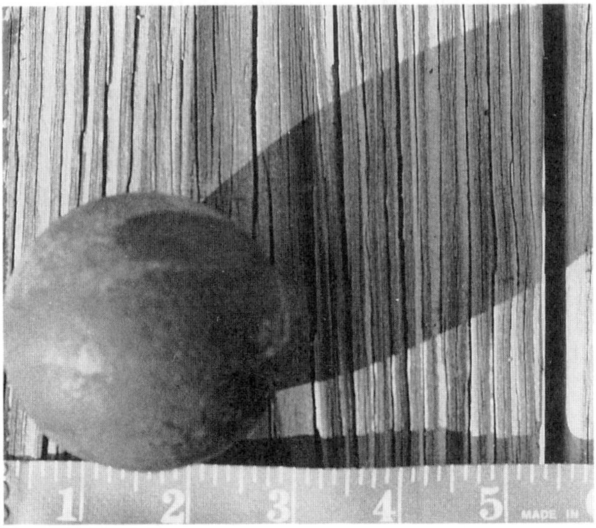

AN ILL WIND

Because the war had started when cannon fired on Fort Sumter, South Carolina in Charleston Bay, Federals always held that city in high contempt. Many, many times during the war, the city was struck with a storm of shot and shell from vessels at sea.

In 1989, Charleston was struck by another storm from the sea; it was called Hurricane Hugo. Rain and high winds turned the area into a disaster zone. There was no food, power, water, or sanitation service for some time. Local emergency crews could not deal with a situation of this magnitude, so a call went out for help for the city. Additional policemen were sent in to prevent looting, and to preserve public order.

Martin Flemming Ring, III was sent from the Columbia City Police Department to aid the people of Charleston. While patroling an area, he noted that the clapboard siding on many houses was at least partially blown away, exposing what had been the exterior of the houses many years ago. While looking at the devastation, he found several solid shot that had been embedded in the walls of the houses; but when the siding blew away, the shot had dropped to the ground. Martin has always been a Civil War buff, and recovering those few solid shot rounds is some of the police work of which he is most proud.

It's an ill-wind that blows no one any good.

Courtesy: M. Flemming Ring, II

THE WARRIOR

Some people believe that our personalities, our attitudes, and the occupations we choose are products of our environment, our society, and our education. But some people seem to be born with a destiny to fulfill. Perhaps his parents knew from his birth where their son's destiny lay. After all, there were two Gen. William Terryes who did great service for the Confederacy. The parents proudly named their son William Terry Slusher.

"I have always loved the idea of being a soldier. Why, even in my youth, I have always had a fascination with guns" said William Terry (who now prefers just to be addressed as Terry.)

This story began in a field in a quiet valley. Peters Creek meanders, splashing clear and sparkling, along the hill known as Greenridge in Roanoke County. Along the hill, there is a deep, cold spring with water that has a robust taste: a taste that beckoned to those who frequently traveled the road in earlier days. Over a century ago, troops that fought the bloody battle of Hanging Rock, less than a half mile away, also stopped.

The Slusher farm was just downstream from the beautiful spring. The spring and the farm surrounding it were owned by Mr. and Mrs. Acorn Strickler. From his earliest years, Terry was frequently in the Strickler kitchen. The house was nestled against the west bank of Greenridge. The kitchen area was made of concrete; and, because it was protected against the afternoon sun, "It was cool on the hottest days." The Stricklers took a liking to their neighbor's boy, and he enjoyed their "lemonade and cookies" many times.

In 1940, Terry was "helping" Mr. Strickler plow the field near the spring. Terry was seven years old and was helping by riding on the back of "Baldy." Baldy was Terry's favorite work horse of Mr. Strickler's team. As the plow turned the rich bottom land, there was an unexpected noise; and Mr. Strickler asked Terry to dismount and see what the plow had struck. Terry scooped the dirt back. What he saw "Made my heart race...I always loved guns and battles since my earliest age," said Terry. He had uncovered a gun from the war. His small hands moved rapidly as he knocked the dirt from the rusty gun.

It was remarkable that the gun stock was in as good a condition as it was after being buried for seventy-five- years.

Terry forgot all about plowing as he moved about the field. "I killed every Indian and Yankee you can imagine with that gun," Terry recalled fifty-one-years later.

Mr. Strickler went back to his plowing, but he eyed the young boy who had the time of his young life. Maybe Mr. Strickler decided then that Terry would be the eventual owner of the gun.

After plowing, Mr. Strickler, Terry, and the gun went to the cool kitchen. Only after cleaning the gun, did they discover the B. McC scratched in the stock. A large "A" was also cut in the stock.

The gun turned out to be rather rare. In fact, there were only 427 in Confederate service. It was made as a Hall Flintlock in the 1820's and 1830's. It was unusual because it was breech loading (most weapons of the time were loaded from the shooting end - the muzzle and the powder and the bullet were tamped in place with a ramrod). At the outbreak of the war, forces under "Stonewall" Jackson captured the Hall rifles at Harper's Ferry.

The rifles were sent to John Barrett's foundry near Wytheville, on August 12, 1862. There they were converted from flintlock to percussion cap rifles. The Confederacy did not have the tools to work with breech loaders; so the breech was "welded" shut, and it became a muzzle loader. Because it was a muzzle loader, it needed a ramrod; so the gun had to be modified. The stock was cut off, and a hanger was attached to the barrel to hold the ramrod.

By February 1863, the 427 guns were returned to the Confederate government for distribution to the troops. Those who used them considered them an excellent weapon. Of the 427, only a handful remain today.

A search of the official records failed to reveal the original owner's name. The following Virginia cavalry units were known to have been on or near Greenridge during the Battle of Hanging Rock: the 14th, 16th, 17th, 22nd, and the 23rd. By checking all available names in those units, the following was obtained: from the 22nd, Private John B. McCraven, Company K; from the 14th, Private Benjamin Franklin McClung, Private B.A. (unreadable) McClung, Private Daniel B. McClung, Private David B. McClung, Private Henry B. (? unreadable) McClung, Private Napoleon B. McClung-all from Company H. The McClungs were all related and came from the Shenandoah Valley. The rifle probably came from one of the McClungs, but no absolute conclusion could be drawn.

It is probable that the gun was discarded at the spring because its old owner had picked up a better weapon from the Hanging Rock battlefield.

Strickler's sons were among Terry's favorite companions. As years went by, Terry was often in their home. Many times, he picked up the wonderful old gun with Mr. Strickler's permission.

Mr. Strickler watched Terry grow and mature and noticed that he had never lost interest in the old gun. It may have shocked the sons when Mr. Strickler gave the gun to Terry. Terry was now fifteen years old, and Mr. Strickler decided that he was old enough to appreciate and take care of the gun.

Some may shy away from military duty; but when the Korean conflict started, Terry was eager to join the Marines. Soon Terry was a "Frogman." How could a boy from the mountains be selected for a Frogman?

Terry said it was all because of his dad. His father had "taught him long distance, endurance swimming as a lad." His father was an inventor, and he took Terry with him to New York City when he worked with a big company. It was a temporary assignment.

When Dad was at the company, there wasn't much to do at the hotel except swim in their indoor pool. A young man who was training in the pool saw that Terry had natural ability, so he started working with him. Johnny Weismuller taught Terry technique. How could the Marines refuse to accept Terry into the Frogman program? After all, he had been trained by Dad and Tarzan!

In Korea, he did reconnaissance diving and also destroyed underwater obstacles. He was then assigned to train other Marines. After the war, Terry continued to ply his trade. He became a consultant to many governments throughout the free world. He helped those governments to set-up their own underwater diving teams. He also formed a company to salvage wrecks from the ocean floor and to explore for mineral wealth.

During his travels, he rubbed elbows with the rich and powerful. He collected many unique and valuable things, but he never lost contact with his roots in Roanoke. The old gun continues to be one of the prizes of his collection.

Col. William Terry Slusher

When his days of world travel ended, he returned to Roanoke and established PSI Industries. He supplies some very unique cleaning agents for commercial and home usage; but at least once a month, the business coat and tie disappear, and Terry is in uniform again. His love, pride, and enthusiasm show in everything he does for the Virginia Defense Force. Under his leadership, the new "Stonewall Brigade" has taken root and grown. Col. William Terry Slusher is now the Commander of the 4th Highlands Brigade. Terry instills morale into his men by recounting stories of courage, sacrifice, and duty. He pulls his war stories not only from Korea to Vietnam, but he never forgets his heroes - Lee and Jackson and the common soldiers who served under them.

Courtesy: William Terry Slusher
PSI Industries Inc.
Box 1127
Roanoke, Va. 24015

Special thanks to Pat Trout & Charles Hagedorn

MAN OF ACTION

They were soldiers, not sailors. In the distant past, the family name was Tand. In their native Belgium the name stood for "Man of Action," and family history remembers that they were hired mercenary - ready to bear arms if the price were right.

One section of the family moved first to Scotland and then to Ireland. In the process, they learned English, acquired a family crest, but lost the original spelling of their name: it became Tant.

While America fought a great Civil War, the Tants of Ireland engaged in a minor war of their own. At times, it is hard to find the truth in inter family feuds; it is impossible to fix fault in the Tant squabble with their neighbors that took place a hundred years ago. It involved women and insults to honor. Insults were traded and blood spilled. It appears the Tants had chosen the wrong family clan to feud with. The other clan were more numerous and very unwilling to seek peace.

The Tant clan knew they could not engage their angry neighbors in an open, fair fight and win. So a nighttime sneak attack was planned. The Tants stole onto their neighbors' property and killed or wounded many of them. They knew that at first light the remainder of the enemy clan would come to their homes and not for a social visit.

According to plan, the Tant clan, all eighty-seven men, women, and children, were aboard a forty-foot sloop and at sea near dawn. The sloop was not designed for transoceanic travel, nor was it supplied for a long journey.

The soldiers were not sailors, but they knew they could not dock in the British Isles. They knew the "New World" was somewhere to the west, so they sailed toward where the sun would set. Apparently, they did not have a compass or know how to steer by the stars.

With little food or water, without skill, on a nonocean going vessel, they sailed west through storm, gale, and scorching sun. To the family name of "Man of Action" could be added "those blessed with dumb luck."

After many days, they saw a land mass. "Safety at last," thought the eighty-seven half-starved Tants. As the Tants looked with eager anticipation at the land, they were being watched by men on another ship.

Before the Tants could reach land, the other ship intercepted the sloop with the order: "Stop, or we'll send you to the bottom of the sea." The men of action stopped dead in the water, and the Union Man of War pulled alongside.

"Where do you think you are headed?" inquired the Union vessel's captain.

"That way- to land," was the reply.

"Like Hell you are!" was the reply. "In case you foreigners don't know it, there is a war going on; and you ain't going to Rebel Charleston."

The non-sailor Tants inquired as to where to go. Baltimore was the nearest port, and it was miles and days away they were told. The Tants asked for food and water, but the Union vessel refused to transfer even a glass of water or a crust of bread. The Union captain gave them only a dire warning of what would happen if they tried to land.

The Tant vessel pulled away from the Union ship. The Tants knew little of the politics of the American Civil War, but the encounter with this Union sea captain had already made them pro-Southern. They knew they were lucky to have crossed the ocean and struck land. They were so low on provisions that they thought they may perish before they made Baltimore. After a brief conference, they decided to sail to Charleston.

It was Ireland all over again: they knew that the enemy clan (the Union ship) was too strong to fight in open water; so they would use their "old friend," the cover of darkness, to overcome their new enemy. They pretended to sail north, but at dark turned south. With the lights of Charleston to guide them, they made port.

There was much immigration between 1861-65, but almost one-hundred-percent of it was to northern ports. The Tants had not received a friendly greeting or been treated fairly by the first Americans they met; they wondered what lay ahead in Charleston. They were overwhelmed. The people of Charleston greeted them with open arms. Food was generously and graciously provided. Very soon twenty-six of the Tant men had jobs. They all got government jobs. The twenty-six were of military age; and they now were in the Confederate Army, fighting millions of men wearing blue. They were told all those blue-clad men were just like the rude captain they had met.

The foreign Tants did good service for their new country, some rising to become non-commissioned officers. When their new country died, it was noted that twenty of the twenty-six were also dead. They had again proved themselves to be men of action.

This is a country of foreigners. Many families came during the war, but only a handful linked their destiny with the Confederate States of America.

Courtesy: John Tant

THE GOOD NEIGHBOR POLICY

East Tennessee had divided loyalties. Many people were pro-Northern, and many people were pro-Southern. Both sides conducted raids, reprisals, and atrocities throughout the area during the war.

A neighbor rode to the Wright farm and excitedly warned the residents that the "Yanks were coming." The kind neighbor then instructed that livestock be driven to a particular valley not far from the house and that the floor of the smoke house be pulled up and the meat concealed below the replaced boards. When the task was finished, the neighbor was profusely thanked by the grateful residents; and away he rode.

As he had predicted, in a short time the Yankee soldiers arrived; but because of the forewarning, the Wrights had no great fear of loss: all was safely hidden.

The Union soldiers did not search about for items to steal but went straight to the valley for the livestock and straight to the smokehouse to pull up boards.

The Yankees stole everything except the hatred that the Wright family carried for their neighbor until they died.

Courtesy: M. Flemming Ring, Jr.

MEDICINE-LOVE-WAR

Huntsville is located in northern Alabama. In 1861, it was a small untamed town: there was still pioneering going on in the area. Unlike back

East, the rules and laws were not fixed or standardized.

Thomas N. Lewis

Thomas N. Lewis considered himself a doctor and had a practice in the small town. When the war came, he knew his services would be needed to treat the soldiers. He volunteered and was accepted by Company I, 4th Alabama Infantry.

The unit was sent almost immediately to help defend Richmond. Lewis soon learned that what was accepted in Alabama, was not accepted in Virginia. Instead of being used as a physician, he was assigned to the Chimboraza Hospital as a steward. A steward was a stretcher bearer. It was even a lower position than a nurse. This war was not treating Thomas as he felt it should.

In September 1863, he was transferred (still as a steward) to the Montgomery White Sulfer Springs Hospital in Montgomery County. Thomas was determined to advance, and he was studying hard to appear before a Medical Board in Richmond. Maybe he could pass and become an assistant surgeon. The assistant surgeon who was his immediate supervisor said that Thomas was studying too hard: in fact, so hard that he was failing to care for the patients. When the assistant surgeon had to prepare the prescription of "cherry bark" and give it to the patient himself, Thomas had studied his last page. The assistant surgeon brought charges against Thomas including insubordination and patient neglect.

Thomas was scheduled to appear before a board, but not the one he wanted and not in Richmond. Thomas's case was to be reviewed by a board in Lynchburg.

Recreation:
Late war-remnants of
Confederate regiment

When Thomas was not waiting on patients or studying, he had been courting a belle from the nearby community of Catawba. It is not clear what she thought of the goings on in Thomas's life.

The board reviewed the charges and accepted the assistant surgeon's (B.W. Bradley) advice. Thomas was a doctor before the war and a steward during almost the entire war. Now, in March or April 1865, he found himself back on the front lines near Petersburg with what was left of the 4th Alabama. Thomas saw his first and last action at the second battle of Darbytown.

The war had not treated Thomas as he thought it would, and now the war had made strangers out of the boys from his home state. He was with them, but he wasn't one of them.

By war's end, Thomas had lost his heart to that belle from Catawba. Thomas didn't get a homecoming welcome in Huntsville. He never became a doctor. In fact, he never left Virginia and the arms of his belle.

Courtesy: Thomas N. Hutson

A SHINY PEBBLE

Someone said memory is like a child walking along a beach. No one knows what shiny pebble or unusual shell the child will choose to pick up and store away in the pocket and which things will simply be ignored. History is similar: one never knows what pieces of information it will reveal and which will be forever lost.

The Salem Historic Society moved the Brown house to Longwood Park and restored it. It is impossible to estimate how many thousands of letters were written and received by people in the house over its long history. In 1991 when a wall of the house was stripped to be restored, one-and only-one of those uncounted thousands of letters was recovered by society member Dr. Warren Moorman. History chose to give us this one shiny pebble.

Williams-Brown House-Store C. 1845-1852

This was only one of the numerous letters Confederate soldier William Brown wrote home. The date is hard to read but appears to be October 25, 1863. The letter was written at Pisgall Church in Orange County. The 9th Virginia Infantry was ordered to prepare the front fortification. The weather was good; the roads were good; and the morale was high. The Yanks could be seen about 600 to 800 yards away. William and the 9th labored around the clock for about three days digging trenches and fixing fortifications for the artillery.

The watching Yankees knew that as the Southern line strengthened, their own line would be less formidable. Because they knew the Rebels were too many and their line too strong, the Yanks decided to talk, not fight. Under a flag of truce, a parlay was held. The Yanks wanted a temporary cease-fire along that part of the lines. The Rebels knew they were in a stronger position - no dice.

After the parlay, to underscore the Rebels' position, the Confederates opened fire on the Yankee pickets, killing seven. The Union boys got the message and moved "to a more respectful position."

Despite this minor victory, despite all of William's hopes, he expressed doubt that the South could win the war. Although William had great reservations about the outcome of the war, he said that the war should not stop until the "Rights of the South" were intact.

William Brown

After writing about the war, William turned to passing news of local interest. Buff Johnson was not looking well at all: he and dysentery were fighting. Fat Sam White was not nearly so fat as he was when he joined the 9th; three days and nights of hard labor will affect a man. Lieutenant Blair attended a prayer meeting and formally accepted Jesus as his Saviour. Since "He professed religion his popularity with the company has increased."

The minds of Privates George Thompson and John Key had not been fixed on Heaven or patriotism, or any high and moral thought. Their captain,Charles Griffen, had been watching the two because he didn't think they were thinking proper thoughts either. Despite the captain's personal interest in the two, the boys went AWOL. Two mounted soldiers were sent to bring the boys back; but as of letter-writing time, Thompson, Key, and the mounted posse were still gone. William said they "will be shot" if found. A search of the soldiers' personal effects yielded letters from both Mrs. Key and Mrs. Thompson. Mrs Key's letter indicated she knew nothing of the desertion. But Mrs. Thompson said she had sold some property to provide money for the escape.

This one letter tells us so much about the person of William Brown, his personal war, and his hope for the future. None of the other letters he wrote home, and there could have been hundreds of them, is known to have survived. History only gave us this one juicy morsel. What a banquet of information history has chosen to ignore.

Courtesy: Dr. Warren Moorman
% Salem Historical Society
Box 201
Salem, Va. 24153

LEE'S NAPKIN

Three of the Boone family never got married. In their old age, John, Emia, and their sister shared a house in Salem.

They were children during the war and grew up in Lexington. Lexington is the location of Washington College (now Washington & Lee University).

After the carnage of America's most devastating war, Lee chose to head that little school in that small town. The great general recalled that some of the happiest times that he and Mrs. Lee had together were during his tour of duty at West Point. Maybe he could find a little peace as president of the college.

The town was full of rumor and gossip as the Lees moved into the president's house. (This same house had provided shelter to Thomas J. Jackson in those happier times before he was known as "Stonewall.") "The Lees were almost destitute, you know," the rumor circulated. They had lost their house and land in the war when the Yankees decided to locate the National Cemetery on their property. There were Yankees buried up to their front door. They had lost everything. Some said the former General "had to borrow proper clothing to take the oath of office" as president of the college.

The Boone family lived near the president's house, and it was little sister who found favor with the old general and new president. Often Lee rode Traveler to town or about campus. Many times, he would hoist the little girl up behind him and give her a ride to school.

To preserve his hat from the stain of perspiration, President Lee would place a cloth napkin over his head before donning his hat. The napkin was tucked out of sight in the front and sides, but sometimes a portion projected from the rear where he could not see. Lee did not see, but the children did. The brother, sister, and other children often dared the young Boone to pull the napkin from under his hat as a prank. Her respect and affection for the great man were so great that, despite the teasing, she never really considered irritating him, the South's hero, even in defeat.

Lee on Traveler
at Lexington
after the war

In those final sunset days of her life, she often thought of her travels and accomplishments. One of the high points of her life was riding on Traveler with a former general who had a napkin stuck under his hat.

Courtesy: Thomas N. Hutson

THE JIGGLING HOLE

East Tennessee was bitterly divided by the war. Many cousins volunteered to wear Union blue and fight their relatives with the Confederate Army. The war raged, not only between relatives in uniform, but between neighbors. There were many atrocities committed by both the armies and civilians against the civilian population. When the war ended for the rest of the country, hatred still raged in East Tennessee. As the rest of the country began to heal, civilians (both pro-Northern and pro-Southern) sought redress for atrocities they endured during the war.

Because Union-occupying forces frowned on such reprisals (especially Southern reprisals), it was best to dispose of the evidence. In Johnson County, Tennessee, there was a sink hole which the locals said had "no bottom." Anything thrown into the hole could never be recovered.

Reprisal parties would sneak warily upon those individuals, civilians, or soldiers who had committed atrocities against them; and then they would kidnap them at gun point and take them to the sink hole. They called it the "jiggling hole."

At the sink hole, a weight, probably a large rock, was tied to the victim's feet. Then as he held onto a large limb, he was swung out over the sink hole. Minutes turned to hours, and the victim's hands cramped beyond human endurance. When it was known for sure that the victim would leave the limb and fall into the hole with no bottom, the reprisal party would ride off as the victim jiggled on the branch. In that way, when the authorities quizzed them, they could reply, "We didn't harm him, and we don't know where he is." The jiggling hole never betrayed their secret.

Courtesy: M. Flemming Ring,Jr.

THE WAR GOES ON!

Over a century later, the pain goes on. In this tale, it is not the story or character that is as important as the storyteller's perspective. The ancestor was not cut from the cloth of sterner stuff: he was no soldier. His motto could have been "If drafted, I will not go; if caught, I will not serve." The storyteller wished for both his name and the name of his not-so-noble ancestor to be anonymous.

When the Southern government sent "Greetings," this man ignored the call. Troops that could be used to fight the Northern aggressor were sent to get this draft dodger. He was caught and taken to Richmond; but he gave himself a discharge from service and ran home.

The telegraph is faster than a man's feet. When the AWOL soldier returned home, he was the guest of dishonor at a "welcome-back-to-the-army party." Soon he was back at Richmond; and, almost as soon, he was back home. Almost as soon he was again a guest of dishonor.

Richmond wasn't his kind of town, and the army cramped his style of life. This going in and coming out was getting to be a dull routine, so he decided to break the vicious cycle. The next time he discharged himself from service, he gave himself a pass not to home but to the mountain near a relative's house.

The welcome-back-to-the-army party went to his home, but he wasn't there to be the guest of dishonor. In fact, it was only after the war that he returned home.

Desertion from the army, Confederate or Union, wasn't unusual; but its effects over a century later are: the war is over. All those who did or didnot serve are gone, but the disgrace of the desertion goes on. This storyteller did not wish his or her ancestor's name known. The disgrace is too much, and the war goes on!

Courtesy: Anonymous

I"LL FIGHT YOU FOUR MORE YEARS

Theodore Felts joined the Confederate Army in Carrol County. Most of the boys from Southwest Virginia served elsewhere. There were large contingents of the mountain boys with Lee, Jackson, or Johnston; but Felts spent many months in his native Southwest Virginia.

For almost a year and a half, he helped guard the critical salt works at Saltville. Theodore watched in the morning as hundreds of wagons filled the road to the "Salt Capital of the Confederacy." The wagons were loaded with wood: firewood had become a critical problem once the Preston Salt Furnace went into full production.

Contrary to what some people believe, the salt was not mined but was extracted from wells. The salt area was flat with much water underground. When mines were sunk in the early days, they simply filled with water; so another system of extraction had to be found. Wells were drilled, and the salt water was pumped out and into large evaporating kettles. Twenty-four hours a day, fires burned under these kettles to decrease the time needed to extract the light brown salt. At the height of production, over two-thousand slaves labored day and night in an effort to supply this critical material for the South. Because of the tremendous need for wood to keep the fires going, mountains near Saltville were stripped of timber: that is why wood was demanded as partial payment for the salt.

Family history has lost the battle, time, and place where Theodore was wounded; but his knee was severely damaged by a piece of shrapnel from a cannon shell. Apparently, Theodore's position was overrun by the Yankees; and he was captured.

After his wound had healed sufficiently, he was transferred from the hospital to the Hell hole, Point Lookout - Prisoner of War Camp. Though wounded and a prisoner, Theodore had not lost his courage or fire. As he was entering the prison, one guard asked, "How long have you been fighting us?"

"Four years," replied Theodore, "and if you give me a gun and a new suit of clothes, I'll fight you four more years." The spirit of the soldier burned bright, but he had already seen his last battle: others did what was left of the fighting while Theodore lingered in prison.

Courtesy: Ruby Padgett

YANKEES MOVE A MOUNTAIN

By the early nineteen hundreds, the war was over in most places; but it still raged daily in the college town of Lexington. "Stonewall" Jackson had marched away from the town to go to war; General Lee had chosen the town to live in after the war.

Kirk Ring was a cadet at V.M.I., and he

recalled that each day the glories and exploits of the two generals and their many followers were recounted for the cadets. Kirk was filled with pride and admiration for the Lost Cause, but a Negro janitor was not. In fact, he had decided that there was more smoke than fire to all he had been hearing. After all, it was the Union-not the South-who had won the war.

When Kirk said something of the glories of the "Old South" to the janitor, the janitor decided to help the Union side with some bull of his own. "See that mountain?" he asked Kirk while pointing to a nearby ridge. "It used to be over there," pointing in another direction. "I was with the Union Army, and we pushed it where it now stands."

Courtesy: M.Flemming Ring,Jr.

Staying Alive

The cold February was warmed by Samuel Lucas's love for Elmira Shelor, and they became one in the Year of Our Lord - Eighteen-Hundred & Fifty-Six. The couple settled in the Childress section (near Riner) in Montgomery County. On a few acres of soil, the two began to build a life together; but four years later, the war would intrude into the lives of all. For the high and mighty, for the lowly and poor, and for those in between, there was no place of refuge. The forming of a nation or suppressing of a rebellion was a process dipped in blood, seasoned with agony, and served with sickness, heartache, and death.

Samuel was married, and he watched members of his family march off to war; brothers Harry and

Charles would never return. The whole Lucas family grieved for their loss and for the losses of their neighbors.

At the first of the war, the Confederate Government was not particularly interested in married men with families; but, as musket fire and cannon shell cut ranks to ribbons, more men were needed. Southern conscription laws made no distinction between married or single, skilled or unskilled.

When Samuel's call came he went-went into hiding. He knew what had happened to Harry and Charles and to many thousands more, and he was determined that it wouldn't happen to him.

With his wife's support, he moved out of the house. Because Confederate patrols or simply units moving through the area might appear at any hour of the day, Samuel had to stay away. If they found a healthy male of military age without papers, it was sure to raise some questions Samuel didn't wish to answer.

Even when the soldiers stole food from his family, all Samuel could do was watch helplessly from the woods. The wife had to maintain the house and do the farming as best she could. At night, she would sneak to the woods to visit and bring food to her man.

Every phase of human existance has a terminus, a juncture, an end: the mountains of bodies, and the rivers of blood that were the war also ended. When the "Cause" was gone, the antebellum South only a memory and ashes, the people of the South glorified the failed war and those who served. When heroes, victories, sufferings, and losses were discussed, Samuel Lucas's name was not mentioned; but he was there to hear the stories. His two brothers, Harry and Charles, and multiplied thousands were not.

Courtesy: Larue L. Wimmer

YANKEE WITH A BAD AIM

Because most of us are descendents of those who fought between 1861 and 1865, the legacy goes on. The present-day descendents have their own personality traits. Some are cordial and nice, and some are not. This story is about the latter.

The man in question was a member of a gun and hunt club. His personality was so that he had run-ins with several members. To say the least, he was not the most popular member of the club.

During hunting season, members would use the club's cabin and spend several days at a time in the woods. At night after dinner, they often sat about and talked and swapped tales.

One evening the-less-than popular member told his Civil War story. After the Battle of Cloyd's Mountain in May 1864, the Confederate Army fell back on Radford to defend the vital railroad bridge over New River.

Remains of New River Bridge

The following morning, the Yankees showed up and started contesting for possession of the bridge. "My great-grandfather was there on the bridge abutment when the Union attacked," he stated. Then he went on to tell of a near miss: a Union minie ball struck the abutment between the ancestor's legs and only two inches below his vital manly parts.

About this time, one of the other club members spoke up, "I wish the Yankee had a better aim: that way, we wouldn't have to put up with you."

Courtesy: M. Flemming Ring, Jr.

AN UNUSUAL LETTER

Uncounted millions of letters were sent during the war. Although many people believe that war letters are a rarity, they can be found by the hundreds in many public and private collections. Some of these letters offer important insights into the war for the historians; others only offer insight into the writer. Some letters have beautiful, flowing handwriting; others are barely or totally unreadable; some use articulate prose with perfect grammer; others are filled with spelling and punctuation errors. Quite often, letters are found that have both horizontal and vertical writing. In the late war, in the South there were shortages of trains and rails, guns and powder, food and clothing, and even paper. Therefore, it was not unusual for the writer to send a letter written along the normal horizontal lines and for the reader to return his letter written vertically.

The purpose of this book is to record tales that are principally oral. Some letters and other written background information are used to verify or enrich the story. The reason it was decided to use the letter to Julia Ann Cruechfield from her husband (who only signed the letter with an "R") isn't because of its content but its appearance.

The letter was written on June 29, 1862, the day of a "big fight." It is not known when Julia in (Sumerfield, North Carolina) received the letter. R. Cruechfield was no scholar as he wrote about the big fight, "Bulets flew all arond my head like hale." (When bullets were fired high into the air and had lost their speed, they did fall like hail. They often struck soldiers on their heads or shoulders but did no major damage.)

R. Cruechfield was a devoted husband, and he started to write his letter as soon as the guns fell silent. Although he did not state it, it appears the battle was a Southern victory. Either the Union retreated or hoisted a white flag so that the wounded and dead could be removed from the field of battle.

R. Cruechfield was not only a good husband; he was a good businessman. During the battle, he "Picked up a pistol off the battlefield...." R. knew his market well. When armies engage and soldiers are shooting or being shot at, a soldier can never have too many guns. R. made a deal with a comrade to sell the gun for $50.00, and R. wanted cash in hand. R. knew granting credit would be foolish. His debtor may not live until the battle's end to pay him. Also, R. knew that the value of his gun would rapidly decrease at battle's end. (It would be a lot like the value of a Christmas tree on December 26.)

As previously stated, R. started writing as soon as the guns fell silent; but he may not have written as much as he had intended. He was interrupted by an officer and told to help those not so fortunate as he. He was detailed to help remove the wounded and dead from the field.

R. folded his letter and placed it in his pocket and went about his grisly assignment. When the letter reached Sumerfield, Julia Ann had to be shocked and deeply moved. Although the grammer left something to be desired, the words conveyed images of smoke, death, horror, and courage; and the blood stains (from some of the dead or wounded her husband had carried) on the letter gave her a graphic illustration of what R. had just come through.

Courtesy: Frank Detwiler, Jr.

SANDS OF TIME

Dwight Jackson made his living with the sweat of his brow and the labors of his hands. He worked building homes to last. He never dreamed that anyone would pay him to play with his hands and to create something that was designed not to last.

It was an accident that led him to this very unusual craft. In May of 1988, Dwight was a forty-five-year-old man. He was on a beach in Norfolk, visiting with some friends when they asked him to babysit their two-year-old daughter for a while. To entertain the child, he joined her playing in the sand.

"It only took fifteen minutes" as he turned a pile of sand into a human form. Dwight didn't think about what he had done until the friends returned. They were astonished at the beauty and detail of his work. Only when they started bragging about his work, did he realize he had talent.

Later that same day on a public beach, he

created his second sand sculpture. When strangers passing by "oohed and aahed" at his work, he knew his friends were not just being kind with their comments.

Dwight's first public exposition came in October of that year when the March of Dimes asked him to do a sand sculpture in a public park in Bristol, Tennessee as part of their fund raiser. That was only the beginning. Since that time, he has been featured in many expositions and craft shows.

Dwight had finished reading my book **The War in Southwest Virginia 1861-65** when he got an invitation to exhibit at the big Labor Day celebration in Saltville. Saltville bills itself as the "Salt Capital of the Confederacy." After reading about the war and now going to a town so important and so fought over during the war, Dwight was determined to make a figure related to the war. "But what?" he thought.

He got his final inspiration from another of his talents and fields of interest, music. "I've always liked drum music...drummers aren't talked about much...but (during the war) they were very important. They called the shots." That is to say, they were the voice of the officer during heavy combat. Because of the noise of cannon and rifles, an officer's voice could not be heard; so the Drummer Boy used the rhythm of the drum, repeated over and over, to tell the troops whether to attack or retreat.

The drummer was quite a challenge. Not only was it a human form but also there were to be a hat and uniform. Sculpturing a detailed drum from sand was hard, "but the hands and drum sticks was something else," he said. The picture doesn't do justice to the monumental work. Visitors stared in amazement.

It took several days and many man hours of patient work to complete the "Confederate Drummer Boy," but Dwight knew that this, just like his other works, would be torn to bits. "It's like watching an historic house being destroyed," lamented Dwight. "I take pictures from every angle because I know that is all that will be left." It is sad to see it destroyed, but the kind compliments, pictures, and knowing he "did his best" is what keeps Dwight looking forward to the next exposition and not back to the last.

Dwight Jackson

As visitors pass the sand sculptures and try to brand the art work with all of its detail into their memory, they also know they are witnessing a unique creation. It's like a rosebud opening, a beautiful explosion of fireworks, or a baby's first step - to be savored to the fullest now because it will never come this way again.

Courtesy: Dwight Jackson
Box 603
Honaker, Va. 24260

TOO LATE

Desertion from the ranks was a major problem for both sides during the war. Fear was only one of the factors that led men to desert. The miserable daily life of the soldier- the lack of food, clothing, shoes, (particularly in the South)- led men to desert the army. The call from the home front might be too great to resist. The lack of manpower to plant and gather crops forced many families into near starvation. With increased Union incursion into the Confederacy and increased desertion, the home front was no longer safe. Many mothers and wives wrote long letters, encouraging their men to desert and come home to feed and to protect them. Many soldiers answered the call.

Desertion was usually punishable by death, and the preferred means was by firing squad. Two Confederate deserters had been caught in Floyd County and placed before a firing squad. As the order to "fire" was about to be given, a rider approached. He bore the message, "The war is over! The war is over!"

The two deserters believed their lives had been spared, but the Confederate officer did not believe the news and gave the command, "Fire." The two deserters died, but for nothing; the war was indeed over.

Courtesy: M. Flemming Ring,Jr.

I SCALPED A YANKEE

The war was over. Mrs. Cumbo of Russell County, was overjoyed when she saw her three sons walking toward the homestead. She was luckier than many women: she still had sons to come home.

The joy was rapidly diminished, and confusion mixed with anger soon took over. "Hy, one of her sons, was wearing the hat of the Union conqueror." How could her son show such disrespect for the "Cause" that they all believed in and many had died for?

Though she hugged her sons, she couldn't keep her eyes off that Union kepi (hat). Soon her dismay was over as the boys explained. After the surrender, the Yankees were kind enough to feed them a meal, even if it was from captured Confederate supplies. All they had to show for four years of their lives were the clothes on their backs and a little food in their stomachs.

It was over: The army dissolved. The three brothers started walking home. The Spring sun was very hot. Two brothers had big slouch hats to protect them from the sun; one brother had no cover. He wished hard for a hat.

As they walked along, they came upon a dead Federal along the road. His pockets were already turned inside out, indicating that other Confederates had stolen any money he may have had; but they didn't steal his kepi. So, the brother grabbed the hat. The Yank had been dead for some time. Not only did the hat come off the Yank, but so did a great deal of the scalp. The men were used to death and dying, so the sight was not repulsive, but common place. The brother simply shook the hair and skin out of the hat and put it on.

Later he would say "I had to scalp a Yankee to get his hat." It is uncertain if the Yankee kepi that came home on a Southern soldier's head still exists.

Courtesy: Jim Lloyd
Lloyd's Barber Shop
Rural Retreat, Va. 24368

BLOOD AND WATER MINGLED

John Felty was born in Wythe County, in 1822. He was thirty-seven years old when the war started. He was never in the regular Confederate Army, but he was a member of the Home Guard. Some members of the Home Guard referred to their type of units as the "cradle and grave outfits" because the units were composed of those either too young or too old for the regular army.

John's unit had little training and had seen little action. In May 1864, Union Generals Crook and Averell launched simultaneous attacks into Southwest Virginia. Crook moved the infantry toward the critical railroad bridge over New River at Central Depot (today, Radford) while Averell advanced the cavalry on the South's last remaining salt works at Saltville.

Home Guard units throughout the area were activated. Some units were sent to oppose Crook, some to oppose Averell. The Wythe Home Guard was sent to protect the Lead Mines at Austinville.

As Crook moved through the mountains, the Confederacy decided to do battle near Dublin, (Cloyd's Mountain). High command decided that the Wythe Home Guard would be more useful at Dublin than at Austinville, so the unit started marching toward Dublin.

For several reasons, General Averell decided to attack Wytheville, not Saltville. Wytheville had no protection, so a courier was sent to the Wythe Home Guard en route to Dublin to turn around and force march back to Wytheville.

Fortunately for the town of Wytheville, Gen. John Hunt Morgan and his band of savage fighters arrived in time to defend their own (Battle of Crockett's Cove), but the Home Guard wasn't there. While massive battles were fought in the Department of Southwest Virginia, while men fought hand-to-hand in desperate combat, while soldiers and generals covered themselves with glory, the Home Guard only got tired and covered by dust.

They marched toward both battles but fought in neither.

John Felty and the Home Guard were called out for guard duty several times over the summer but not to do battle. By late September, the Confederacy had good intelligence indicating that Union Gen. Stephen Burbridge would attempt to destroy the Confederacy by destroying Saltville. Without salt, the South could not transport food by rail (because food would spoil), thus the Confederacy would be doomed.

Burbridge advanced from Pikeville, Kentucky, with 5,200 well-equipped soldiers. The South had little to oppose him. The Home Guard units as far east as Salem, were activated and sent to Saltville. At Saltville Home Guard and regular army units formed a defensive line. It was a weak line; of the approximately 3,200 Confederates, 1,300 were Home Guarders.

At 9:00 P.M. on October 2, 5,200 well-equipped Union soldiers started an assault on 3,200 poorly-equipped, some poorly trained, Southerners; and John Felty was on the line. By 12 o'clock noon, Felty and his Home Guard unit were in the thick of the fight. A massive Federal attack on the South's right was taking its toll. Men fought hand-to-hand. The ground was covered with the dead and wounded. The Confederate right was anchored by two regular army units that had seen much action. Under murderous Union fire, the regiments were forced back. Now, only John Felty's unit of the Home Guard stood between the Yankees and total victory. At every action during the war when regular Union Army units clashed head-on with Confederate Home Guards, it was the Home Guard who lost.

Union forces turned their full strength on the Home Guard unit in their exposed position. Bullets flew thick and fast. Men fell in agony. The noise was deafening, and smoke choked the air. But the poorly-trained, poorly-equipped "cradle and gravers" took all the Union boys could give and held the line. A sure Union victory was turned into a Union defeat. John Felty's unit had taken more casualties than any other Confederate unit that day, and the Home Guard had outfought the regular army for the only time during the war. John Felty may have been happy, but the sight of so many men he knew lying dead and wounded must have preyed heavily on his mind.

During the night of October 2, General Burbridge retreated. John Felty and his unit were sent to guard in case the Yankees decided to return. John and a neighbor named Wilkerson were to guard near a corn field. As the sun rose, so did John's thirst. No Yankees had been seen all morning, so John assumed it was safe to go to the spring for a drink. But sometimes free water has a high cost.

Shortly after John went for a drink, a Union cavalry unit came in sight. Wilkerson saw the Yankees but could not warn John without exposing himself. Wilkerson hid in some newly-shocked corn. The Yanks rode past and did not notice him, but they did notice John drinking from the spring.

The water was clear, cool, and sweet. It made quite a noise as it gurgled and splashed- so much noise that John never heard the Union horsemen who rode up behind him. The Yanks did not ask him to surrender but in cold blood shot him through the back. John's blood flowed into the clear, cool, sweet, spring water.

John Felty - March 24, 1822 - October 3, 1864.

Courtesy: Mac Felty

HOT SHOT

We have often heard someone called a "hot shot," meaning either that person is better than, or thinks he is better than, other people. That phrase, like so many others, comes through the war to us today.

The war saw the first engagement of iron-clad naval vessels, but "hot shot" belongs to the era of the wooden ship. Shell refers to an exploding cannon projectile; shot refers to a solid projectile - thus non-exploding. Fire on board a ship is the worst peril a sailor faces. Hot shot was designed to increase that peril. Before an engagement, solid shot was heated red hot over an onboard-ship furnace. The cannon was loaded, and extra wadding was rammed down the barrell as a buffer between the gunpowder charge and the hot shot.

Shortly before firing, the red hot "hot shot" was rammed down the barrel. When the gun discharged, the hot shot would penetrate the wooden hull of the enemy vessel. Because of the extreme heat of the hot shot, any burnable material that came in contact with the shot would likely catch fire. Because one cannon blast could contain a number of hot shot, fire was likely to occur in several places at once within the enemy ship.

Hot shot was considered more devastating than non-heated shot; therefore, a "hot shot" is better.

Courtesy: M. Flemming Ring,Jr.

JUST ASK HER FOR THE GOLD

The following account belongs to several families. All agree the location is on Chesterfield Mountain in Grayson County; but none agree to the exact origin of the story. The only areas of agreement are that it involved a husband and wife and an army payroll and occurred toward the last of the war.

The facts as to which army's payroll it was are disputed. Whether it was in gold or paper (Most people now believe it was gold), which side of the war the husband and wife were on, and who was responsible for the atrocities that occurred are also in dispute.

By applying a little historical knowledge, I believe we can make some reasonable suppositions. Because the husband and wife (whose names have been lost in time) handled the payroll and because they lived in a Southern area, it is safe to assume it was a Southern payroll. Because it was a Southern payroll in the late war, it would almost be a sure bet it contained only paper money: (1.) The South was desperate for gold. (2.) Soldiers were always paid with paper, not gold. Because of vile atrocities committed, it probably was not the invading Yankees but bushwhackers and deserters who committed the dastardly acts.

As the war lengthened and casualties rose, desertion became a major problem for both armies. A deserter's life was not worth much: if caught, he would probably be shot by a firing squad. To avoid the authorities, deserters from both sides sought refuge in the rough mountains along the Virginia-North Carolina border. Here they formed gangs and hid. They preyed on the civilians (particularly women) on the farms. Assault, thievery, and brutality were trademarks of a band of deserters.

The most likely scenario is that a brave man who was in charge of the Confederate payroll of paper money (not gold as many today believe) got word that a band of deserters was coming to steal the money. He was in the area of Chesterfield Mountain but not at his home. To protect the payroll, he buried it.

The rumor was true, and he was soon the prisoner of a band of deserters. They demanded that he tell them where the payroll was, but he refused. They began to beat him with their fists and when he went down, to kick him; but he still refused to talk. He knew that once they got the payroll they would kill him anyway. They may have used a bull-whip to lash the poor man. Apparently, the beating he received burst some vital internal organs; and he soon died.

The deserters felt no sympathy for his pain or sorrow at his death. The only sorrow they had was that he carried the secret of the burial spot for the payroll to the other side. The deserters decided that he wouldn't have buried the payroll without telling someone he trusted where it was buried. Who would a man trust more than his wife? Some of the deserters in the band came from the area and knew where the dead man's home was on Chesterfield Mountain, so away rode the group.

It was surprise and shock combined with terror that the payroll master's wife felt when she saw the gang of deserters coming. She was a young and attractive woman with long, flowing blonde hair. All agree that she had a long, white dress on that day. She may have run from the band or tried to bolt the door, but she did not escape.

The deserters caught her and demanded that she tell where the payroll was buried (Some say she knew; others say she did not know.) Either way, she didn't give the information. They told her that her husband had died because he wouldn't tell and that she had to tell or she, too, would die. The horrible news tore at her heart, but no information was given.

Because the payroll master had died too quickly before they could torture him, the deserters knew better than to brutally beat his wife. Her hands were tied and raised in the air; her long, white dress was ripped from her body; she was slapped, whipped with a bull-whip, and burned on various parts of her body! The torture went on for hours. It must have seemed like an eternity before merciful death reached out to her and took her while the sky was light. If she knew where the payroll were hidden, she did not tell the bushwhackers. For their acts, they received nothing on this earth; but they did reserve a place in the lake of fire that burns forever on the other side.

The story does not end here with death but only begins here. From the end of the war until present day, a woman dressed in white with long, flowing blonde hair has been seen many times on the mountain. Most unexplained sightings of ghosts occur at late night or in low light. Ghosts are only seen for a fraction of a second in a haze or shadow; but this woman's appearance is always in full light, and she remains for some time. She never speaks, but locals believe that she wishes to: once she can tell the secret she died for and has kept for over a century, then and only then can she rest.

With this in mind, she has approached people on the mountain; but none have had the courage to ask. Although many have seen her, few would talk to me about what they saw. People of good character would tell me what they saw and felt only on the condition that their names not be revealed. They were concerned that people might think they were unbalanced if they said they had seen a ghost.

"I have lived in the area all my life, and I had heard the story since my youth," said a man with white hair who will never see his sixtieth birthday again. In his youth, he had moved up the mountain along a logging road. He moved almost one hundred feet off the road up in the dense trees and sat down quietly. He was dressed in brown clothing and shielded by some undergrowth. He was there to hunt squirrels and did not want them to see him before he saw them. He was as quiet as possible as he listened for the squirrels.

As if from nowhere, he saw a woman walking on the logging road. She had long, blonde hair and wore a white dress. "I knew who she was right away. I knew she could not see me from the road because I was well hidden in the trees." She walked up the road until she was exactly parallel with the hunter. She turned from the road and started up the hill toward him. As soon as she turned, she looked the hunter straight in the eye

(All of the storytellers agree that she looked them in the eye and that the stare caused fear).

When she was on the road, he seemed to recall seeing the dress move as she walked but not when she was coming up the hill. He wondered if she were walking or floating. His eyes were transfixed on hers. The undergrowth and hill did not change her pace, nor did she appear to be a ghost but a real woman. With every foot she moved toward him, the fear increased. His heart raced, and sweat began to flow. He knew that all he had to do was say, "Where's the gold?" and she would tell him. Though she made not a sound, he knew she wanted to speak. He could be a rich man if he would only ask her.

The hundred feet became fifty and then twenty, and then she was only ten feet away. The terror was too much! He had his squirrel gun in hand when he leaped from his position and started running as hard as he could. He didn't stop until he was out of breath. When he looked back, she was not there. That was the only time he ever saw her and the only time he could have asked her for the gold.

In a more recent sighting, a lady who lives on the mountain was washing dishes when she looked through the window toward the garden. There in her garden was a lady with long, blonde hair and a long dress of white. "What's that woman doing in my garden?" she thought.

She went out the back door to investigate. As she rounded the corner and looked toward the woman, the woman was staring directly into her eyes. There was "something unnatural" about her eyes, and it frightened the homemaker. She stopped and stared back for a moment, but fear compelled her to return to the house for safety.

Back inside, she returned to the window to look again at this woman with the unnatural eyes who shouldn't be in her garden. When she looked, the woman was gone. Because her field of vision was so great from the window, she knew it would be impossible for the woman in white to have run completely out of sight in so short a time. Only then, did she realize what she had seen.

The lady in white is most often seen in the woods. A hunter was moving through the forest when he came to a clearing. There in the clearing was a woman in a white dress. She was lying on the ground. Her blonde hair was radiating out from her head in an almost circular pattern. Once again, the woman stared directly into the hunter's eyes. It took only one look to scare this man with a gun in his hand, and he started running from the woman.

Recently, a boy drove his girlfriend to a secluded spot on the mountain (to do what lovers often do). From out of nowhere, a woman with blonde hair and a white dress rode past the car on a fast-moving horse. Within an instant, she returned and was directly in front of the car. The horse reared high in the air, and she stared directly into the boy's eyes. In terror, he reached for the keys to start the car to get away. In the split second it took to glance at the car's dashboard, she simply disappeared.

Locals also tell of a musical band from Taylor Valley. They were a country band who decided to take some publicity pictures in a natural setting, so they drove to the mountains. Using trees, undergrowth, and streams of water as backgrounds, they took a series of pictures. No, not a one of them saw the ghost lady; but when the pictures came back, they all did. In one of the pictures, the lady in white with long, blonde hair is sitting near the band beside a stream.

There are those who say that some people's souls get stuck between Heaven and Hell. Because they have something they must accomplish on this earth, something that they didn't accomplish while alive, they must remain until their destiny is fulfilled. If that is so, let us hope that her next appearance will be her last: that someone will ask "Where is the gold?" so this woman tortured in life can at last find peace in death.

(Courtesy: Of some of the people who frequent Jim Lloyd's Barber Shop in Rural Retreat, Va.)

Green Cannon?

After the war, cities, towns, counties, and private groups (like the United Daughters of the Confederacy, the Grand Army of the Potomac, and United Confederate Veterans) began to erect statues and plaques to honor those who fought and their cause.

Cannon became a highly prized decoration on court house lawns across the country. When the cannon were rolled into place, they represented great power on the battlefield. By modern standards, they seem like "pop guns." Most people think they are a quaint oddity.

Once the cannon were in place at the court house, it became the duty of the county to maintain the guns. Some cannon were made of iron and had to be coated with shellac to prevent rust damage. Some were made of bronze or brass. During the war, they would have been kept shiny by the gun crew; but county workers are not gun crews, and the guns aged.

The jailer at Fincastle (Botetourt County) kept eyeing the cannon on the court house lawn. He knew something was wrong. Everybody knew that cannon were not green, but this cannon was. (As bronze or brass oxidizes, it turns green).

The jailer and some of the inmates were heading toward the cannon with black paint and big brushes to rectify the situation. The County Administrator saw what was about to transpire and called out, "What are you doing?" The cannon is still green.

Courtesy: M. Flemming Ring, Jr.

First Yankee Captured

Edward Pendleton Hayth's family lived near Fincastle; but he may have enlisted in the Confederate service at Buchanan. He was known for his horsemanship and daring; so it was natural that when war came, he would join a cavalry outfit. Before war's end, he would rise to the rank of lieutenant in the 2nd Virginia Cavalry.

Although in many battles from the start of the war until the bitter end, Hayth won his fame early on in the war. When the boys were young and gay, and the war was still a game and not a deadly business, the 2nd Virginia was on picket duty not far from Washington City.

The Federal cavalry was equally as green as the Confederate's. Apparently, a brave boy in blue rode too far away from his lines; and Hayth sighted him. Hayth, vowing to capture the Yank, mounted his horse. The other members of the 2nd

Virginia watched as Hayth stalked his prey. When the Yank was as far away from his own lines as possible, "Like a cyclone," Hayth pursued him, firing his pistol as he went. The surprised Yank was soon holding up his hands saying, "Don't shoot, I surrender."

Hayth disarmed his prisoner and returned to a hero's welcome at camp. The men of the 2nd Virginia clapped and cheered because Hayth had "captured the first Yankee on Virginia soil."

Courtesy: Roy Hayth

Lt. Edward Pendleton Hayth
Co. C 2nd Va. Cavalry
(Late war drawing done around the camp fire. Hayth in a captured Union officers coat.)

Horse Trading

Hayth met the Yankees many times on and off the battlefield. During lulls in the fighting, warriors often met as friends and did some serious trading. Southern tobacco was in great demand by the Union troops. The Southern boys longed for the taste of coffee which was in very short supply because of the blockade. So, men who tried earnestly to kill one another during the day often met at night to barter.

Little is known of the exact transaction between Hayth and one of his counterparts in the Union army, but each soldier rode off on the other's horse when the dealing was done.

Within hours of the deal, Hayth knew that he had gotten the better part of the trade when his horse, with no rider, came back to camp. Had the Union rider been shot? Had the horse bolted? Had the Confederate horse refused to serve with the Northern army? No answer was given, but it was clear that Hayth had swapped one horse and now he had two.

Courtesy: Roy Hayth

Song Swap

Jim Lloyd is a member of a musical band, the Konnarock Country Critters, so he is very much interested in music.

"Everybody knows," he said, "that after the battles, soldiers often swapped tobacco and coffee; but they also swapped music."

He went on to explain that after the

fighting, when the armies were close together, bands would often have a musical duel across the river. Union and Confederate bands would try to out-perform each other. "Dixie Land" might be countered with "The Battle Hymn of the Republic." "Camping Tonight" might get a Southern response of "The Bonnie Blue Flag." The songs of the day were also played. Opposing bands would capture the enemy tunes they liked and use them at a later date.

"There are even records that show that along with the tobacco and coffee that were exchanged through the lines, sheet music to songs were also traded."

Courtesy: Jim Lloyd
Lloyd's Barber Shop
Rural Retreat, Va. 24368

Don't Let Me Die With My Boots On

"War! War! War!" was the cry that echoed throughout the South in April 1861. James Madison Howard, like thousands and thousands of others, answered the cry. Everyone knew that it would be a short, glorious war and they would be the new patriots: the new heroes, the founders of a new nation.

James was well educated, married, and rearing a family in Floyd County, when he marched off to war. Because of his education and standing in the community, he was elected Second Lieutenant in Company B, 42nd Virginia Regiment Infantry.

For most who signed up for this short, glorious war, it became a long, bloody, dirty affair; but, for James, it was short. He was wounded in the foot at the Battle of First

Manassas. The pain of being on his feet, marching for hours, was more than he could endure. So after little more than one month's service, he was forced to resign and return to Floyd.

2nd Lt. James Madison Howard
(In Virginia Militia Uniform
Floyd Blues Company)

Back home in his community, he tried to resume a normal life; but the pain persisted. Despite the pain, it appears he became a member of the Home Guard unit and saw limited tours of duty during the war. Whether on duty with the Home Guard or about his community, he often remarked, "Don't let me die with my boots on."

Four years after the firing on Fort Sumter, South Carolina, the war was winding down. The Confederacy was collapsing. A portion of Gen. George Stoneman's command (3rd Brigade under Col.

John Miller) pushed into Southwest Virginia. It was almost certain the mounted troops who entered Floyd County on April 2, 1865, were from the 3rd Brigade.

James joined a group of Home Guards, determined to hold the town. When the smoke cleared, Floyd ws in Union hands; and James, the father of three, lay dying. A soon-to-be-free black man whom locals affectionately called "Old Uncle Wise" performed the last earthly kindness for James so that he wouldn't slip into eternity with his boots on.

Courtesy: Waller L. Howard

A WET CONFEDERATE

As the war lengthened and the South's ability to maintain large armies decreased, Confederate commanders were forced to rely more and more on Home Guard units. The Home Guard was composed of young boys, old men, and those not physically able to stand the strain of regular army life. They were civilians with little training. They provided their own arms (Many used flintlocks or squirrel rifles). The area commander could call them to active duty to supplement his regular troops when the danger was imminent and local. Robert Porter was a member of one such unit in Wythe County.

The last raid into what was the Confederate Military Department of Southwest Virginia occurred in March 1865. The raid started from the Knoxville, Tennessee area and was commanded by Gen. George Stoneman. Stoneman commanded approximately 10,000 mounted infantry and cavalry troops. They were among the best troops in the Union Army. Because all the men rode horses, they could travel very rapidly.

From Knoxville, they moved on Boone, North Carolina. There the crack Union troops decimated the Home Guard units that defended the town. Stoneman then separated a brigade of his army and sent it north toward Mount Airy, North Carolina. The brigade's mission was to enter the Department of Southwest Virginia and to destroy the mines at Austinville. Austinville was the South's only source of lead. Then the brigade was to attack and burn Wytheville (for the third time during the war). After accomplishing these goals, the unit would head east and destroy bridges along the Virginia-Tennessee Railroad. This would eliminate the Confederacy's only east-west rail link in the upper south.

Confederate commanders knew Union forces were on their way but did not know their number or exact intentions. At Hillsville the Union column surprised and overwhelmed a small unit of Confederate cavalry (dismounted).

The Southern commanders now knew that the Yankees' target was the mines. In that area, a call went out to all Home Guards to move to defend the mines.

Robert Porter lived about four miles from the lead mines in a section known as Porter's Crossroads. He and other men rushed toward the ferry that would take them over New River to Austinville on the south shore of the river. When they reached the river, they knew they were too late. The Union force was busy destroying the mine facilities. There would be no more lead from these mines for the Confederacy.

The total number of the Home Guard unit may have been fifteen or less, but the men would oppose the Union forces when they attempted to cross the river. There was some brief firing by the Home Guards, but it was soon decided that there were too many Yanks and too few Rebs to continue the fight. The Home Guards were told to disperse and find positions along the road where they may be able to fire on a Yankee from ambush and then flee for their lives. Porter and three or four other men decided if they were going to fight it would be near their homes, so they moved rapidly over the road toward Porter's Crossroads.

The Union column crossed the river. The Yanks knew the few Home Guards could not stop them, but they were apprehensive that they may be gunned down from ambush. At least part of the Union troops moved toward Porter's Crossroads. At some distance ahead, they spied Robert and the others. They spurred their horses to full speed in an attempt to catch them.

Union Cavalry pursuing fleeing Rebels

Apparently, Robert and the others (all on foot) saw the Yankees at the same time the Yankees saw them. It was a foregone conclusion that horses could out-run men, so the group left the road and scattered into the woods. Robert hid in the lush, spring undergrowth near the road.

The Union column rode rapidly to the area where they had seen the pesky Rebs and halted, but they could not see or hear any Rebels. The commander then ordered a private to shinny up a tall tree to have a look about. In minutes, the private reported from his high perch that there were no Rebs to be seen. "Okay" said the officer, "climb down."

Now the Union column had been riding for some time without a rest break. This private decided to empty his bladder before climbing down. The yellow liquid coursed through the air and splashed on the lush, spring undergrowth that concealed Robert Porter.

Every fiber in Robert's body wanted to jump from the ground and blow that rotten Yankee out of the tree, but he knew that the price of revenge would be his life. So Robert just lay there, caught in an unexpected Spring shower.

Being wounded in battle is bad, but it does endow the soldier with the pride of bravery and courage. Being peed on carries no such honor. It was a long time after the wet Confederate had dried off before he could see any humor in the situation. Only then, could Robert tell people about the greatest and worst day of his military career.

Courtesy: James Porter

Honor & Dishonor

Most men who enlisted, whether in Yankee blue or Confederate gray, considered themselves Christian gentlemen of principle. They joined the service because of patriotism, the desire for glory, self-sacrifice, and to protect the people and things they loved. Robert Wright was one such

Brig. Gen. William E. "Grumble" Jones

Major Gen. David "Black Dave" Hunter

man.

Robert was a cavalryman who probably served under Gen. William E. "Grumble" Jones until Jones's death in June of 1864. Robert was then attached to Gen. John McCausland's cavalry.

Noted national commentator Eric Sevareid has remarked, "Wars are often fought for moral principle; seldom conducted by such." War changes men. Men who had knelt in solemn prayer with their families now found themselves torching fine Southern mansions. Men who considered themselves fine gentlemen found themselves carrying off the last ham from some poor Northern farmer's smoke house. Atrocity begat atrocity.

Gen. David "Black Dave" Hunter laid waste to the Shenandoah Valley in the Spring of 1864. Confederates under John McCausland burned Chambersburg, Pennsylvania in retaliation. Robert Wright was there, and he did a soldier's duty.

War's end brought Robert back to his native Washington County. Leaders, both Northern and Southern, urged the population to put the war behind them and start rebuilding the nation. Robert had been a low-ranking officer but decided the war was over. He would rejoin the Union. He went to the court house to take the Oath of Allegiance and become a voting citizen again.

It was then that Robert discovered that all the talk about putting the war behind him and starting a new life was only talk. It was okay to put Union atrocity behind, to forgive and forget, but Southern atrocities were neither forgotten nor forgiven. Because he was a part (a very minor part) of the burning at Chambersburg, he was denied the right to vote.

Robert Wright could not rejoin the Union: he was still a Confederate. He remained a citizen of an occupied country until his death.

Courtesy: M. Flemming Ring, Jr.

THE DESERTER

Thomas Stuart Walker accepted his father's gift of land but rejected his offer of a slave or two. There was no room in Thomas's marriage for slavery.

Thomas Stuart Walker's first born was Thomas Fowler. He and his brothers often visited their grandparents' slave-holding household.

Thomas Fowler married and had his first child shortly before the war. Thomas was living in Tazewell County, when the war erupted. Tazewell County's northern boundary would later be part of the southern border of West Virginia.

Thomas was exempt from the first draft laws, Northern or Southern, because he was married and overage. Despite being exempt, Thomas's feelings were stronger than ties to family, farm, or life. He joined the Second Kanawha as a private. The Second Kanawha entered Confederate service as the 36th Virginia Infantry.

Because of his education and accomplishments, Thomas rose in rank to first lieutenant. Rank carries certain status and privileges, but some of the jobs required are very distasteful. Lieutenant Walker got some good news and some bad news. He was getting a furlough to return to his mountain county to visit his wife. The bad news was that he must capture and bring in a deserter.

Walker knew desertion was a big problem for the army and anything to slow desertion would be a big help. Walker knew he was the best man for the job. He knew the deserter personally, knew his family and relatives, and knew where the deserter lived. In fact, they had both enlisted in the Second Kanawha together. Yes, he was the man to capture this dirty, low, despicable deserter and friend. He was the best man to drag him away in front of his family's eyes and back to the army-there to be the focal point of a firing squad.

The journey from the Shenandoah Valley to Tazewell County held no joy. He was a soldier, a man of honor, an officer, and a patriot. He must do his job. He was a friend of the deserter; the families knew each other.

Walker had killed men in battle. Those men only had faces and bodies: they had no names, no past. The death of this deserter was a different matter all together. He didn't have to talk to those boys in blue that he had shot down. What would he say to this deserter friend and his family? What could he say to relatives from both the deserter's family and his own family when the war was over and years had passed?

As he moved toward Tazewell County, Walker came up with a scheme which he felt would satisfy the army and the deserter- one with which he, too, could live.

Upon reaching the community where the deserter lived, Walker went directly to a general store which also served as a post office. It was an early hour of the day when Lieutenant Walker arrived to do his official business, and he let everybody know what that business was. Walker probably knew some of the customers by name: but whether he knew them or not, he told all that he was there to capture and return the deserting neighbor to the army.

It was a late hour of the afternoon when Walker left the store for the deserter's home. He was sure that by this time someone- friend, neighbor, or relative- had gotten word to the deserter that Lieutenant Walker was on his way. Walker dutifully searched the house, the barn, the outbuildings and grounds. He could truthfully report to the army that he could not find the deserter.

When the war was over, Walker felt no guilt for his actions; and this working furlough may have been satisfying and fruitful. Lieutenant Walker added two children to his brood during the war years.

Courtesy: Jim Walker

I DON"T WANT NO PARDON

Jacob Lester Hale was born at Elk Creek, in February 1825. He came from a long line of "livers." His grandfather passed away at age 116, and his father lived until he was 95 years and 7 months.

Private Jacob Hale

With the first shot fired at Fort Sumter, war fever raged throughout the South. The boys from Grayson County, decided to form a company, and no ordinary name would do. They decided to call themselves the "Grayson Dare Devils." Jacob was 5 feet 10 inches tall, with blue eyes and auburn hair; and, at age 36, one of the oldest members of the company. Jacob told the enrollment officer that he was a farmer who could neither read nor write.

He was healthy enough, and he marched off with the rest of the boys. The company lost its snappy name and entered service as the 4th Virginia Infantry. They became part of the famous Stonewall Brigade.

Being illiterate stopped Jacob from rising in the ranks, but it did not keep him out of combat. He was wounded in the cheek near Spotsylvania in 1863; and in May 1864, he found himself on the line there again. An overwhelming early morning Union attack crushed the Stonewall Brigade in what was later called "Bloody Angle." The brigade commander, Gen. James Alexander Walker, was severely wounded in the arm and was carried off the field. He was one of the lucky ones: so many men were killed, wounded, and captured that day that the Stonewall Brigade passed into history.

Jacob was captured and marched off to the "Ice Box" of all Union Prisoner of War Camps at Elmira, New York. The cold wind that swept off Lake Erie chilled men to the bone, and the Federals refused to provide proper clothing and blankets. Food was scant; but the jeers, taunts, and torture from the black guards wasn't. The harsh treatment left many Southern boys dead, as evidenced by the vast cemetery there. The harsh treatment left many Southern boys who survived with a deep hatred for anything Northern.

At war's end, Private Jacob Hale was offered release if he would take either of two pledges: he could take the Oath of Allegiance to the United States; and, because he wasn't an officer, he would be released and become a full citizen again.

This oath Jacob refused. He did pledge never to bear arms against the United States again and was released in June 1865.

Jacob returned to Grayson County and was a member of the Methodist-Episcopal Church-Southern branch of course. He never voted or had any privileges of citizenship in the land of his birth. To his death, he refused to request a pardon and to end his war with the United States of America.

Jacob would probably have agreed with the words and thoughts that one of his fellow Confederates penned after the war. The song went in part:

"I'm just a good old Rebel,
Now that's just what I am.
And for this fair land of freedom
(meaning the U. S.)
I do not give a damn.
I fit against it,
I only wished we won.
And I don't want no pardon for anything I done.."

Courtesy: Dave Robbins

IT TAKES A WORRIED MAN TO PET A ROCK

War history exists in family lore, battlefield parks, libraries, museums, and in the ground. There are those who study the war by digging through dirt to uncover bits and pieces of metal that help tell our ancestors' stories. These people use hand-held metal detectors which they pass over the ground hoping to hear a signal that indicates the presence of metal. They call themselves a variety of names: "relic hunters," or just "hunters," or "diggers." Or if they wish sophistication, they are "artifact recovery and identification experts." Those who have never hunted for relics this way may visualize a man, a machine, a level, grassy field, and every dig a success.

Pat Trout has been at this hobby, sport, obsession, for over ten years; and he tells a different story: "I can't count the times I have tripped or fell when my footing gave way on the side of some steep hill. I've sprained my ankle, skinned my knees and elbows. Briars have cut me and bugs have bitten me... I wish every hole I dug had a relic but they don't. I have dug all day and come home dog-tired with less than five bullets. I have stumbled into yellow jacket nests by accident, but they stung me on purpose. I have even had copperhead snakes strike the coil of my detector...like to have scared me to death."

One day Pat got a "good" signal. He was thrilled because he believed he was about to dig a belt buckle (one of the most prized trophies a relic hunter can find). Hurriedly, he dug down; then the earth caved in, and there stood a growling groundhog. "Almost bit me," recalled Pat.

Pat wanted very badly to go after that potential belt buckle, but he considered the groundhog's strong defensive position (inside a three-foot-bunker); he considered those sharp white teeth and the groundhog's version of the "Rebel yell." Then Pat retreated. "Whatever it was, is still there." This "Civil War battle" was won by the groundhog.

Not all days are bad. Pat has retrieved hundreds of bullets of many calibers and designs. He proudly displays belt buckles, artillery shells (or fragments), bayonets, and gun barrels. All these things are made of metal, enabling his detector to pick up their signal. One of his most unusual finds gave off no signal- It was a rock, but not an ordinary rock.

People in the 1800's believed that one could get rid of tension by rubbing a stone. They were called "worry stones." There are those who may

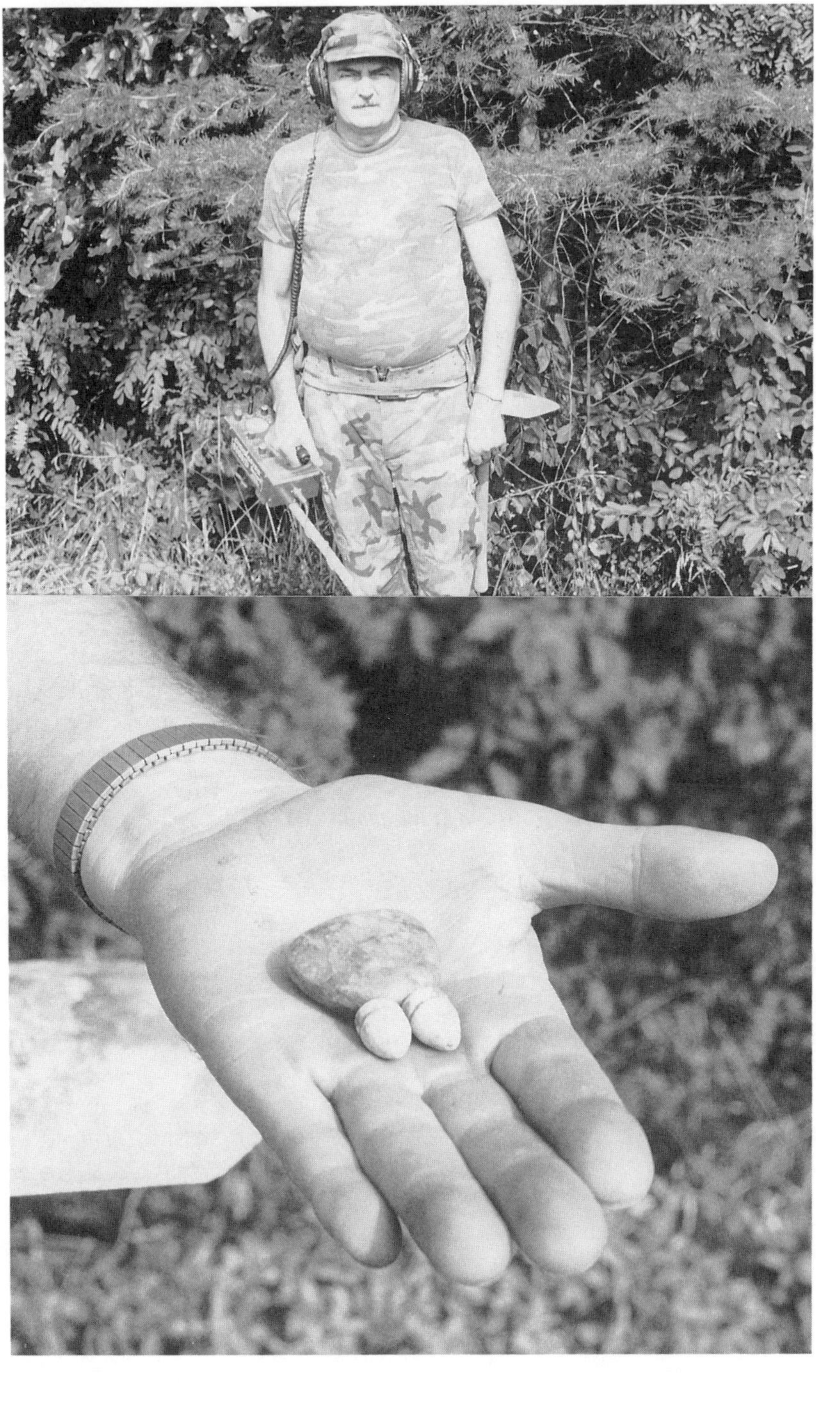

Pat Trout

scoff at the medical value of a rock. They may relegate it to useless folk medicine or characterize it as "snake oil," but there does seem to be a need to focus energy generated by tension to one physical point for relief. It is not uncommon to see a person under great mental strain wring his hands. Where other than battle would there be more tension? Where could a worry stone be put to greater use? The smoothness of the rock indicates the soldier released a lot of tension through it.

On that cold December day in 1987, Pat was searching a battlefield near Amelia Courthouse. He was not surprised when his machine signaled metal below. He wasn't surprised to retrieve two 44-caliber colt pistol bullets, but the worry stone was a serendipity for Pat. Now in a huge showcase surrounded by massive metal relics, sits one small rock.

Like many finds, this one raises as many questions as it offers answers. It was found on the Union side of.the battlefield, but that does not absolutely prove it was owned by a Union soldier. Why were two pistol bullets and a stone dropped at the same time? Nothing else was recovered in the immediate area to shed light on what had happened.

There are those who downplay the role of relic recovery in the study of the war, and there are abuses in the field; but, without recovering objects, we would never know of some incidents that did occur.

The 19th Century is gone, but the worry stone has not completely died out. Even today, some gift shops sell the rocks at fifty cents each. There is even a twist on the worry stone principle. These are stones in dainty cloth sacks called "prayer rocks." The cost may be a little higher; but, by rubbing them and asking for help, the user is put in touch with a higher authority.

Courtesy: Pat Trout

WHITE TO BLACK TO WHITE TO BLACK

Religion and politics have generated more debates, arguments, and wars than any other subjects. The two men who sat on the porch of the President's house, President of Washington College that is, were not part of the mainstream of Lexington society. Both men were "outsiders," intellectuals, and considered as "peculiar" by most of the town's people.

Professor Thomas Jackson was born in the far western part of Virginia. He had graduated from West Point and served in the War with Mexico. Jackson was dogmatic, authoritarian, and inflexible in his views. Many locals said that these were the reasons Jackson had resigned from a promising army career and had come to teach at the small college of Virginia Military Institute. Not only were Jackson's ideals inflexible, even in walking or sitting he seemed inflexible.

The man seated in the other chair had earned a doctorate degree in religion. He too was an outsider. George Junkin had moved with his family from Pennsylvania to become President of Washington College. Junkin was assertive. Some locals said he was abrasive and pushy. He had heard some locals say, "We don't care how you did it up North."

Both men were very moral, religious, and principled; but they didn't see eye-to-eye on many subjects. Slavery was an emotional subject that was sure to generate heated debates between the two men. Professor Jackson attacked Doctor Junkin in his field of religion and scored a big verbal victory. Jackson forced Junkin to admit that the Bible has many references to slavery from Genesis through the New Testament: that God had not condemned the institution but had used it to characterize the relationship that should exist between man and God. It could be considered a "Christian institution," and, if God had created it, then it was not up to man to question or condemn it.

Junkin was forced to accept the institution of slavery intellectually, but he told Jackson he could not bring himself to own another human being. Jackson said he could!

Junkin loved Jackson like a son but at times may have wished to have thrown Jackson off his property; but he couldn't because the men had one thing in common that would prevent it: Junkin's daughter Elinor was Jackson's wife. When Elinor got married, Junkin didn't lose a daughter; he gained a son and Jackson moved in with Junkin.

Both families attended the Presbyterian Church. Junkin opposed slavery emotionally but did nothing for the colored people. Jackson favored slavery but felt he had a special mission to the colored people, both slave and free.

Jackson decided he would start a Sunday School for the colored people. He would educate them and show them the way toward Heaven. State slave laws forbade the assembling of slaves and discouraged education; but Jackson reasoned that when the laws of God and man conflict, the law of God would prevail. Initially, the Presbyterian Church did not endorse Jackson's efforts; but Jackson continued to bring the coloreds to Sunday School anyway.

Many colored people were interested in the afterlife that Jackson spoke of. There would be no master or servant and no work to be done. The Presbyterian Church saw that Jackson was doing good and fulfilling a need, so the church began to support Jackson's work. Members of the church were encouraged to send their slaves to Jackson's Sunday School. John Fuller and David Hopkins were friends and members of the church, so they enrolled their slaves in Jackson's Sunday School. Hopkins owned the mixed-blood slave Ella (Ellen), but Fuller leased her.

Ellen was among almost one-hundred colored people (slave and free) that Jackson taught. Another slave in Jackson's Sunday School was Lylburn from Jackson's school - V.M.I. These two slaves would later marry, but that's getting ahead of the story.

If it hadn't been for the war, Jackson would have died an unknown man; but the war changed everyone's life. At the first sound of war, both Jackson and Junkin left town. Jackson marched off to Richmond at the head of the Corps of Cadets; Junkin and part of his family went to Pennsylvania.

At the first big battle on Virginia soil, Thomas Jackson lost his first name. From then on, he was known as "Stonewall" Jackson. Jackson became a national hero overnight. The townspeople of Lexington who had always thought he was peculiar and had considered him to be an outsider now were so proud of their hometowner.

"Stonewall" Jackson

Shortly after First Manassas, the Pastor of the Presbyterian Church received a letter from their member, now the great "Stonewall." He did not open the letter but assembled the congregation to hear what Jackson had written about the great Southern victory. Everyone was shocked that the letter contained no references to the mighty battle but only Jackson's money for the support of the colored Sunday School.

In two years, Jackson fell wounded on the field of honor. Death did not conquer Jackson. He welcomed it and was glad that he would meet his Savior on a Sunday. His last words were, "Let us cross over the river and rest in the shade of the trees."

The North rejoiced; the South mourned; and Lexington received the body of her adopted son. The colored community wept for Jackson as it could for no other Southern general. The members of Jackson's Presbyterian Sunday School felt a personal loss. Many members vowed never to forget this man.

Slave marriages were not recorded, so we don't know when Ellen and Lylburn "jumped over the broom." They had a son also named Lylburn in May 1862. The younger Lylburn had older and younger brothers, but he outshined them all.

At war's end, the South had lost everything except its pride. The Jackson-Junkin debate about slavery was a moot question now because the institution no longer existed in the United States of America. But the institution may not have been as hateful and cruel as many believe. The 1870 census reveals that a Fuller lived on property owned by a Hopkins; and on this same property, the former slave Ella (Ellen) and her family lived.

In 1870, Ellen said her son Lylburn could neither read nor write; but he was going to school. Although officially abolished, a bond remained between former slave and master. The Presbyterian Church and Jackson's colored Sunday School continued. Ellen didn't forsake her Lord or the man who opened the way for her and for other members of the colored community.

Now that Ellen and Lylburn were free people, they needed a last name. Unlike many former slaves, they did not take a former master's last name. It is not known why they adopted the name Downing.

Jackson's former sister-in-law was Margaret Junkin. She married John T.L. Preston who, like "Stonewall," taught at V.M.I. The Prestons, of course, kept up with the goings on in Lexington and the Presbyterian Church. John was the Sunday School Superintendent. This brought the Prestons in contact with the Downings. The Prestons were impressed with a middle son also named Lylburn. He learned to read and write in a short time. He was well mannered, showed that he was very intelligent, and had a desire to succeed.

Jackson was dead, but his spirit lived on in Lexington. There were now a large number of little "Stonewalls." It was very common in those early days after the war for many children, both black and white, to be named "Stonewall."

Lylburn no doubt played with some "Stonewalls." He also heard about the great man from his parents, the Prestons, and many of the townspeople. Lylburn often visited the plain gravesite of the general. As a youngster, he recognized that the final resting place of "Stonewall" should have an appropriate monument. He determined at a young age that he wanted "...to erect a monument worthy of the illustrious benefactor of the colored people of his town."

When the Prestons heard of this former slave boy's dream, they took even more interest in Lylburn. "What do you want to do with your life?" asked the Prestons.

"I want to help my people by becoming a doctor," was Lylburn's reply. The Prestons applauded Lylburn's desire to help his fellow man.

Lylburn did not become a doctor. He said he felt the hand of God directing him and the call to the ministry. "He was obedient to the heavenly vision, abandoned his own preconceived ideas of what he wanted to do in life, and with singleness of purpose consecrated himself to the ministry." When Lylburn told the Prestons of his change of plans, they were thrilled. John felt that his Sunday School training was at least partly responsible for Lylburn's decision.

John was a professor at V.M.I. His wife Margaret was the educated daughter of an educated minister. The Prestons were determined to help Lylburn become an educated pastor. The Prestons said they would help finance Lylburn's education.

The name of the college that Lylburn chose to attend (and where Preston money was sent) appears at first glance to be a slap at everything the mighty "Stonewall" fought for. Both Lylburn's and the Preston's money went to Lincoln University in Pennsylvania. Until he was assassinated, President Lincoln was the most hated person in the South. With war's end, "Reconstruction" began. Reconstruction was a code word for continued war without bullets. The South's assets were now owned by Northern "carpetbaggers." The state governors were appointed by the President. Most people could not vote. The laws were enforced by an army of occupation. The Southern people furnished cheap labor and raw materials and were forced to buy goods produced in the North. Southern resentment of reconstruction was so strong that the people of the South voted against it for three-quarters of a century; the solid-Democratic South voted against the conquerors-the Republican Party.

When the population of the South learned that Lincoln had wished to readmit the Southern states to the Union without harsh reconstruction, the dead Lincoln's image improved greatly in the South. Now the Prestons could send their money to a school that bore his name and not feel as if they were being traitors to the South for which they fought.

Lylburn went from Virginia to Pennsylvania to school. The money the Prestons gave was a big help, but Lylburn also had to work part time at a hotel to earn enough to continue school.

During summer vacation, he returned to Lexington to help his benefactor, John Preston, with the Sunday School which "Stonewall" had formed. One summer, the American Tract Society paid his way to America's resort city - Atlantic City. Lylburn was sent to evangelize, but he also socialized. Here he met Dr. and Mrs. James I. Brownson who were vacationing from Washington, Pennsylvania. Before the summer was through, Lylburn and James had formed a close friendship. When Lylburn returned to school, both Preston and Brownson money went with him. He no longer worked at the hotel.

The summer at Atlantic City was a good one for Lylburn; he met a girl from another religious family. Lottie Jackson Clinton was the daughter of Bishop J.J. Clinton of the A.M.E. Zion Church. Love grew between the two. When school was out in 1888, Lylburn rushed to Atlantic City to marry Lottie on the third of June.

Lylburn did not just get an A.B. Degree in 1889. He graduated with the highest of honors. For four years, he had the highest grade average in his class.

After graduation, he continued his education in the Theological Department. He also taught Latin to undergraduate students. In 1889, he completed his training for the ministry and received a Bachelor of Sacred Theology. The school did not want him to leave: if he would stay and teach, he would have a permanent position and steady income. The offer was attractive, but Lylburn's vision called him to preach to the people, not to lecture to college students. He had to decline the offer and follow his vision.

By the time Lylburn graduated, his boyhood dream of an appropriate monument to "Stonewall" was a reality, (The grave of Jackson now had an immense monument next to it.) but Lylburn had plans. Sometimes youthful dreams do not die with age.

The bright new Presbyterian Preacher received job offers not only from the school but also from growing, prosperous churches. Members of those churches couldn't believe that Rev. Downing had turned them down for a church that offered him only $2.00 a week salary.

Lylburn and Lottie moved to the railroad town of Roanoke. Lylburn may have had some doubts as to the wisdom of the move when the first Sunday's take was only 67¢. Lylburn's church was nothing more than a small missionary work. They had no money. They had no proper building. But with 67¢ in hand, Lylburn was determined to have a self-supporting congregation and a proper church building.

Lylburn sought and got aid from the "Freedman's Bureau." Many white Southerners resented this government agency and considered it another part of reconstruction. Sometime during this era, Lylburn officially became a Republican.

Reverend Downing showed his can-do spirit could make things happen. His church membership did grow and prosper. The congregation sent him as a delegate to their General Assembly three times. He became moderator of the entire Presbyterian Synod of Catawba. He reached outside the church to the black community, and his success showed in each endeavor. He became a Grandmaster of the Masons of Virginia and District Grandmaster of the Odd Fellows. Also, he was active in the Pythians.

The 1800's were dying, and a new century was being born. Ideals of the 1800's were disappearing. In a desperate attempt to find a moral basis for continued war against the South, Lincoln had turned to the slave issue (when the war was half over). As the 1800's died, Northern support for Southern Negroes was almost gone. Northern businessmen were more interested in assets that the white people in the South controlled. Northern politicians were more interested in courting the Southern white vote. Reconstruction was gone. Whites regained the vote and control of the legislators. Throughout the South, "Jim Crow" laws were passed to deny the black population the vote (and thus political and economic power).

Confederate veterans began to downplay or completely forget the vital role Southern blacks had played during the war. With white men in the trenches, it was the black men (slave and free) who produced the food and worked in industry. Slaves by the thousands helped build the fortifications. Many black men worked in hospitals or served their master in the field. A large number would enter the trenches and fight alongside the white soldier before the war was over. John Brown died believing that the slaves would rise up and murder their white owners if they had a chance; but throughout the war, the vast majority of the slaves remained loyal; and no mass uprisings occurred.

Most white people in the South could not accept that former slaves could be their equals. The belief that skin color was a measure of worth was not confined to the South but accepted throughout the country. Many people believed there was a need to control the Negro population and keep the black "in his place."

Laws and economic factors were used to make the blacks secondary citizens. Sometimes mob violence ruled. If a Negro man were even suspected of raping a white woman, he may be strung from a tree. Although most lynching of Negroes in the early part of the century occurred in Northern states, it was not unheard of in the South. Even Roanoke experienced racial violence during this period.

Against this backdrop, Rev. Lylburn Liggins Downing saw the need to extend a hand of understanding from the black community to the white, just like Jackson had extended his hand to the black community. He became the only Negro on the city's Republican Committee. He was a member of the committee to record the history of Roanoke soldiers in World War I. He became the city's first probation officer and worked to help keep Negro youth in school.

By the 1890's, the church building was up; but it was not complete. 1906 was a red-letter year for Lylburn. His old alma mater recognized his achievements and awarded him with a Doctor of Divinity Degree. The long dreamed of church was

now in the final stage. Lylburn was going to make the church more than a building: it would be the fulfillment of a dream of the past, a vision for the future, and a visual symbol of the present.

The church would show that Lylburn had not forgotten but was still grateful to those who had helped him. With pen and ink, Lylburn set his ideas on paper; but it took an artist and the skilled hands of Tiffany's studio craftsmen to fulfill the dream. In 1906, the Fifth Avenue Presbyterian Church would be completed; and Lylburn's windows were dedicated.

The arched center window was flanked by two smaller windows. These beautiful stained glass windows were dedicated to Col. John T.L. Preston and Doctor & Mrs. James I. Brownson in recognition of their generous contributions to a poor, colored boy from Lexington. The large center window was reserved for Professor and General Thomas Jonathan "Stonewall" Jackson. In this window, Lylburn's youthful dream came to fruition ("...a monument more worthy....").

By Lylburn's design, the sun's rays make the stained glass sparkle on a scene from the Shenandoah with mountains and a stream. A cabin, a camp, and soldiers on the move recall the essence of Stonewall country. The scroll across the base of the window reads, "Let us cross over the river and rest in the shade of the trees."

On that day in 1906, the white community grasped the black hand Lylburn had extended to them. The United Confederate Veterans were present. Witnesses like Major Henry Trout, Col. S.S. Brooks, and E.W. Speed delivered orations and words of appreciation to Rev. Lylburn Downing and the colored church. The main speaker was "Uncle" Jeff Shields. The "uncle" was a title of love and respect he received during his days as a slave. Although slavery was gone, he proudly retained the title and his claim to fame. He was the personal servant of the mighty "Stonewall" during the war: a position of honor in both the black and white communities. The news services carried the story to the nation and the world. Lylburn would receive many letters of support from this country and even from England.

The "Stonewall" Window

Lylburn crossed over the river in 1936. His legacy was too great to be consumed by death, and this story has only brushed on parts of it. Lylburn left a love of education to his children and grandchildren. They were highly educated- most graduated from college; some received doctorate degrees.

In 1960, Lylburn's church burned. The two small windows were destroyed and Jackson's main window was damaged. Most of the window was restored and moved to behind the altar in the front of the new church. The church itself was moved. You will now find the Fifth Avenue

Fifth Avenue Presbyterian Church

Presbyterian (the first and only colored Presbyterian church in Roanoke) on Patton Avenue.

But the story has not ended. The work Jackson started is still living. In recent years, the Fincastle Rifles Camp-Sons of Confederate Veterans (descendents of those United Confederate Veterans) commissioned an art work to be done that featured Lylburn's window to honor Jackson. With members of the church and Sons of Confederate Veterans looking on, Mayor Noel Taylor (the first black Mayor in the history of Roanoke), flanked by the Confederate and United States flags, accepted the work on behalf of the city. The City of Roanoke has chosen to display that art work in its main library.

The hand that Jackson extended to the black community before the war is still a bridge over

Mayor Noel Taylor

which both races can meet in friendship. Let us hope this story has no end.

Courtesy: Eloise D. Allen

Dorthy C. Kate

Alphonso J. Preston

Fifth Avenue Presbyterian Church
301 Patton Avenue N. W.
Roanoke, Virginia 24016

I SWEAR ON A PLUG OF TOBACCO

As one turns off the old highway and onto Sulpher Springs Road outside the small community of Chilhowie, one is confronted by an immense two-story house with big, cool porches that sweep the sides of the structure. One could easily mistake the house for an antebellum plantation manor. One could visualize the master watching his slaves at work and viewing the town in the distance, but the house dates from the turn of the century.

Pendleton House

At the door, the visitor is greeted with big smiles from Russell and Mary Ann Martin; and they say, "Welcome to Pendleton House." The Martins have worked for years to restore the mansion. They have poured more than money and sweat into the old house; they have also poured love, and it shows in each corner. The Martins are very sociable people; and, as the restoration neared completion, they decided that they wanted to share their dream house with others. They wanted people who would really appreciate a visit to the past to come and lodge with them, so the Pendleton House Bed & Breakfast was born. They like people who are not in a great rush to get from point A to point B. They like to cater to those who really enjoy getting in a porch swing under a huge sun roof, sipping a mint julip, watching the sun go down while a cool lilac-scented breeze blows by.

Russell likes to tell the visitor about propping up sagging porch columns and replacing fallen plaster the way craftsmen of days gone by did it.

Mary Ann delights in showing off the antiques throughout the house. She is very pleased when people "ooh and ahh" over pieces of her collection. The Martins point out the difference in the ornate architecture in the "receiving portion" of the house (living room, parlors, and guest bedrooms) and the plain bedrooms used by the family.

During the tour, the guest is shown an object that seems so out of place among the glitter of brass and copper and the rainbow of light emanating through cut glass. In the midst of sparkling chandeliers, sets a block of brown tobacco; but the Martins value it as highly as the most costly antiques. The plug of tobacco has so many memories to the Martins, and Russell loves to tell its story. It is a link to the past and an avenue to the future.

"To understand the importance of this antique, you have to go back to the war (Between the States)." Russell recalls for the visitor some of the many battles fought in the area, of Union raids and thievery, of the breakdown of law and order and home-grown thievery. "Southern money was no good, and nobody's property was safe. Gold, silver, salt, and tobacco were the only things that kept their value during those turbulent times," recounts Russell. People had to hide their valuables. Some treasures were hidden so well that they were never recovered.

In Glade Spring, a small community near Chilhowie (Both communities are near Abingdon.), a resident hid his store of tobacco behind a "false wall" in the cellar. For reasons unknown, the tobacco was forgotten.

In the autumn of 1933, Russell's grandfather Samuel Rhudy got the contract to install a new furnace in the old house. After sixty-eight years of darkness, the forgotten tobacco (a very large store) saw the light of day. Mr. Rhudy asked the owners of the house about the tobacco, but none of the Keys family could supply information.

It was decided that because Mr. Rhudy had found the tobacco, he would receive half of it. Mr. Rhudy was a man who loved history and family. From 1933 until his death, he dealt out the tobacco to his children and grandchildren one plug at a time. He told each the story and history behind the tobacco; and then, before he would give it to his offspring, he required a solemn promise. They had to promise to take care of the plug and pass it on to one of their offspring. The tobacco could never be given to a non-family member. The tobacco could never be sold. The children to the fourth generation still keep their word and pass the plug on.

The Martins have talked to their children about the tobacco and the sacred vow. They feel confident that the promise to Samuel Joel Rhudy will be unbroken into the next generation.

After hearing Russell speak, the visitor knows why the Martins prize the old plug of tobacco as much as any sparkling, costly antique. When Russell sees the tobacco, he remembers the

war, his grandfather, his father, and his link to the future through his children.

Courtesy: Russell & Mary Ann Martin
Box 1127
Chilhowie, Va. 24319

STILL HOLDING THE LINE

It looks like a joke and a novelty. The Confederate cut-out soldier holds a plastic sword high with his "on to victory" sign. He is ready to do battle with his cannon made from a piece of pipe with a portion of drain hose over the end of the barrel. Yes, the cannon balls are really painted baseballs. The cut-out still stands guard on the Hess property in Roanoke.

Robert Edward (named for Robert E. Lee) Hess, Sr. built the mock cannon in the 1950's and often fired smoke bombs and small powder charges. Sometimes the noise got him in hot water with the local police, but he kept firing the cannon.

The practical-joke cannon has a history that is older than the United States. In fact, the Revolutionary War was the beginning that led to a fake cannon and a cut-out soldier with a plastic sword on a hill in Roanoke.

The Hess family can trace their history to the state of Hess in what is today Germany. That state furnished the British with mercenary (paid) soldiers to help suppress those upstart colonists. The Hessian troops were among the most feared and hated troops that the patriots fought against.

As you know, those upstart colonists threw the British and most of their hired guns out of the colonies and established the United States of America. Not all of the Hesses went home. Part of them settled in Pennsylvania, part near present-day Stuarts Draft. Though separated, both parts of the family have remained in contact from the revolt until this present day.

When war severed the nation, cousin Hess shouldered a rifle to kill cousin Hess. Aquilla Hess of the Virginia Hesses was approximately eleven years old when the war began. Apparently, he tagged along with some of his older brothers or cousins and saw one of the first battles near Winchester. At the battle, the Hesses held a bloody family reunion. Some of the Northern cousins had reason to wish they had never attended. Aquilla went to the hospital after the battle and ministered to his wounded Northern cousins. They were not happy that their Southern cousins had helped gun them down, but they were very grateful for the help their Southern cousin Aquilla gave them.

The world had changed, and the once-close family would never be the same: they were related by blood, and a common heritage, but "being family was no longer enough."

Very few eleven-year-old-boys knew as much about battle, wounds, and pain as Aquilla did. The experience did not frighten him but only strengthened his young, Rebel heart. Most people practice firing a gun to sharpen their aim for hunting animals and as a pastime. Aquilla practiced with a more serious intent. It was said that he "could shoot the eye out of a turkey at

100 yards." By late 1864, the war had grown old; Aquilla had grown older; the Confederacy accepted men who were younger; the blood letting continued. Aquilla became "one of the youngest sharpshooters of the war." Aquilla showed his bravery and skill. Through his actions, many holes were filled with men dressed in blue.

Recreation:
Young Confederate boys in training

The war ended, but the family rift never completely healed. War memories were transmitted through each family. Aquilla's deeds and the goals of his country were remembered and passed on mainly by Elmer Thomas Hess. Elmer's love of history was transmitted to Robert Edward Hess, Sr. who passed it on to his sons John and Robert, Jr. Robert,Jr. refers to himself as "the lone Rebel."

The war started the animosities between the Northern and Southern branches of the family.

Inheritance disputes and differing political ideals have resulted in a kind of cold war among some members of the families. Some members even refuse other members' requests just to see common heirlooms from the family's rich history.

These circumstances along with Robert, Sr.'s love of his Southern past, led him to construct the pretend cannon and place it on his property "to protect his land from the Yankees" (including some members of his own Hess family).

The gunfire ceased over a century ago, but the war goes on; a lone, cut-out soldier and his fake cannon still hold the line.

Courtesy: John L. Hess

WHY?

In the Spring of 1861, the air was so full of excitement that one could almost cut it with a knife. The war fever raged all over the South land. Speeches, cannon's blast, new uniforms, and gleaming swords were everywhere. From the big cities to dusty, county crossroads, men and the women who loved them cried, "Southern independence!" and "War! War! War!"

In the mountainous county of Grayson in Southwest Virginia, A.M. Davis was forming his company of men. One of the first in line was Joseph B. Cox. He strutted around proudly in his new uniform. He showed his family and friends his long-barreled pistol. "I am a member of the best unit in the whole army, the Grayson Dare Devils. I'll be a hero when I come back home," thought Joe. "If I die, it will be a glorious, brave death on a field of honor. My death will mean something. I will be remembered for my great deeds." The people cheered as the Grayson Dare Devils marched out of town. Joe was a proud Sergeant with the unit.

In less than three months, the Grayson Dare Devils (now Co.C, 45th Virginia Infantry) were at Lewisburg, (W) Virginia; but Joe wasn't with them. In less than three months, Joe was back in his home county. He had seen no great battles. He did not return a hero. No one would remember his name. He marched off to war to cheers; he was greeted by sobs on his return. His death meant nothing. One can only imagine the thoughts of family and friends as they looked on the casket containing Joseph B. Cox, farm boy, wrapped in a sergeant's uniform.

"Why?" was the question. "Why did Joe die for nothing?" Joe couldn't speak, and God didn't speak. A letter home said it was "the fever." A courier brought Joe's personal effects and $55.56 in back pay.

"Oh Joe," was the heart-wrenching cry. "Why? Why? Why?"

Courtesy: Michael Phipps

TWO DOLLS FOR TWO DOLLS

The Bible says that when a man and woman marry they are no longer two but one. In 1852, William Richard "Dick" Jennings married Mary Johnson Glass, but the two didn't completely become one. What she brought to the marriage was still "hers," and some things were considered "his." She brought slaves, household furnishings, horses, and harnesses to the marriage. They were, by no stretch of the imagination, poor struggling newlyweds. At the same time of the marriage, Dick paid cash for a 1,000 acre farm which they considered "theirs."

By 1854, they had another "their thing," a son. Dick must have been proud to have a son to carry on with the rich family heritage (from both parents) and to be the rich keeper of all that lovely wealth.

Everybody knows that the Confederacy was born with a big fireworks display in Charleston Harbor, South Carolina, in April 1861. Dick and Mary made some fireworks of their own two months earlier. When the Confederacy was born, Mary was two months pregnant.

Recruiting stations sprang up everywhere as the South formed a new government and an army to protect it. No one would have felt badly toward a land owner, slave owner, and a father with a pregnant wife if he didn't volunteer his services to the "Cause," but there were Dick and his horse in line. The Catawba troops became Co. H, 3rd Virginia Cavalry, and Dick and his horse were there. Dick left his things and their things with her things and marched off to war.

Dick, like almost everyone, Northern and Southern, thought it would be a short, glorious war. They would all be heroes and patriots, home before the snow fell.

Dick was at First Manassas. He was proud to serve under the South's first great general, Pierre Gustave Toutant Beauregard. The Yankees called it Bull Run, and the Yanks did run; but the war would not stop running.

After Manassas, Dick felt it to be an honor to be transferred to serve under another general with three first names, James Ewell Brown Stuart. Stuart's cavalrymen felt that they were the cream of Southern troops.

On November 1, 1861, Dick became a father for the second and third times. Mary gave birth to twins whom she named, and Dick knew nothing of it. In January 1862, Dick's unit was resting and regrouping near Lynchburg when an old family friend congratulated Dick on the birth of his

William Richard Jennings

daughters.

Dick went to see the big man himself, Stuart, and asked for a furlough to see his newest family members. Things were quiet, and no action was foreseen in the near future. Dick could go home, but he would have to report directly to Stuart before he left. Dick didn't delay in packing, but there was some delay in seeing Stuart. When Dick finally got an audience, Stuart gave him written permission and a surprise present-twin dolls for his twin girls. Dick's personal pride in the army and his respect for Stuart grew bigger with each horse step toward home.

Dick burst into the house with smiles, hugs, kisses, and dolls for the daughters he had never seen. One can imagine his cooing over those little girls and bragging about how they would be the two most beautiful belles in the whole Confederacy.

Mary told Dick what she had named the twins, but we don't know exactly what was said or the discussion that followed. Mary was probably upset that Dick wanted to call her two little, innocent girls "Beauregard and Stuart." Mary was probably not in favor of giving up the beautiful feminine names she had picked out. Dick may have compromised and said that the two generals had six given names and that his girls could, too. The discussion is unclear, but the outcome is clear. The girls' middle names were substituted. The first born drew the name of Dick's first commander, Ella Beauregard, and the second born became Lillie Stuart.

The furlough was ended, but the war was not. Dick rejoined his unit and the war. As the girls grew in size and strength, the Confederacy declined in size and strength. The number and depth of Union invasions increased.

It was probably the Spring of 1865, and the "Cause" was dying. It is unknown why Dick was at home while his comrades continued to fight toward the bitter end.

There was a rumor that the Yankees were coming, so Dick sent his slaves and horses to hide on the farm at "Buzzards Roost." Mary did the same with her horses and slaves. Mary then went to the basement and dug a hole in the earthen floor. Mary's silver service was buried. She didn't want damned Yankees gorging themselves with Jennings food, served on her things. The crude Yankees often took the silverware with them when they left.

War or no war, it was Spring; and the ground must be broken, and the corn planted. Dick proposed that the horses and slaves return to start the planting. "Fine," said Mary, "you bring your horses and slaves; mine stay at Buzzards Roost."

Dick's slaves and horses did return. The Yankees came. Dick left. He was a Southern soldier, and the Yankees didn't care if he were home or not. If caught, Dick would be killed or captured. The Yanks didn't get Mary's horses or slaves but they did take Dicks - including the harnesses for the plows. The horses were for mounts; the slaves would become soldiers (like it or not), and the harnesses were an extra.

"Where is the silver?" demanded the Union officer.

"We don't have any," lied Mary. The soldier told Mary that he didn't come from the cabbage patch. One glance at the house spoke of elegance. There was a silver service. The Yank said he wasn't going home as poor as he was when he entered the army. The Yankee officer cocked his pistol and placed it against Mary's head and asked the same question again. This time Mary gave a different answer, and her silver service rode off with the Yankee officer.

That night at the Union camp, Dick's former slave couldn't get comfortable enough to sleep. He rolled over and over until he could not be seen by the firelight. He made one fast stop and then left the Union camp. He was a Southerner and loyal to his master. He did not want to be a Union soldier.

The next day he came to Dick and said, "Master Dick, I couldn't get the horses; but I brought you some of the harnesses."

Dick was very grateful for the loyalty and for the gift of life. Without the harness, the plow could not be pulled. Without a useful plow, there would be no crops; and the family may go hungry. The slave whose name is lost in history knew exactly what he was doing when he re-stole the harness.

Dick survived the war, and so did the dolls.

Pringle Myers
decendant of
William and Mary Jennings
at the grave of
William Jennings
with one of the dolls

Courtesy: Lillie Trent

WOMAN OF ACTION

Julia Ann was born a Strout (pronounced Stout). She grew to be a stout woman. She was tall, big boned, and very muscular for a woman. (A descendent refers to her as an "Amazon woman.")

The great Smoky Mountains could be viewed in the distance from John Aquilla Moore's parents' home in Carter County, Tennessee. John also viewed the stout Miss Strout. Before the war, he changed her name to Moore.

By the time war came, there were more Moores. Aquilla's birth was followed by Kate's. When the war came, the nation was divided; East Tennessee was divided; and the Moores were divided.

John, like most men across the South, joined the Confederate Army. Most men marched off to a very "iffy" future at the front. John never carried a gun or saw a battle. He marched away from the front. He went to one of the safest spots in the Confederacy. He went south to Walnut Cove, North Carolina. The arm John bore for the Confederacy carried a hammer. He was a blacksmith. While men from his area died, he made horseshoes, nails, and iron kettles.

While John worked, protected far from the front, Julia Ann and family were in the front. Battles were fought nearby, and neighbor turned against neighbor in East Tennessee. The wife saw more action than did her man. It is not known how much John and Julia saw each other during the war. There were no more Moores born to them during that time.

Because of war shortages and John's absence, it is believed that the farm declined badly. There were probably raids and lootings by both sides against Julia and her young children. By March of 1865, the Confederacy, along with John and Julia's world, was collapsing.

Just like most people, Julia was frightened and dismayed by the crumbling. She decided to be with her man to face together whatever was coming.

Art work by: Willard Gayheart
Box 605
Galax, Va. 24333

Descendents say she "gave" the farm to John's brother, the Reverend Bob Moore. "Gave" may have more meanings than one. "Gave" could have been a figure of speech; the price was so low that she practically "gave" it away. Bob may have paid her in the national currency which wasn't worth a cent in less than one month. Therefore, she would have "given" the farm to Bob. Whatever "gave" meant, it included the livestock, except one horse. Everything that John and Julia owned, along with two children ages six and four, could be carried on one horse.

A brave woman and two small children headed east on the "Rock Road" (today, Route 11). Every turn was frocked with potential danger; each bit of news was bad. Julia moved by day and begged lodging for the sake of the children by night. Although no one had much, her request was never denied. People opened their homes and shared what little they could with her.

She moved east until she got to Wytheville. Here she turned south on the Raleigh-Grayson Turnpike heading toward North Carolina. Although she expected trouble each second, none occurred until she was at or near Iron Mountain.

How she spotted the approaching Union troopers is not known, but it is clear that she knew about their presence- but they did not know about hers. The quick thinking Julia ducked under a bridge, and the Union cavalry horses rumbled over her head. (This only confirmed that the South was collapsing as Northern troops ranged almost at will.)

Julia was worried about her personal safety and that of her children, but she was in dire fear for her horse. She knew that both sides were desperate for mounts. She knew that womanhood and two innocent children wouldn't even slow a soldier who was desperate for a horse.

Julia, Aquilla, and Kate had made it into North Carolina- but not to John- when she was told that there were Yankees on the road. Where was safety to be found? An unknown family opened their doors, literally, to Julia, kids, and horse. To prevent the horse's discovery, the animal was put in the cellar until the danger had passed.

Julia Ann and the children made it to Walnut Cove and John before the Confederacy breathed its last. Together, they saw the Confederate flag replaced by the United States' flag. They faced the world together. There was no farm in Tennessee to return to, so the family simply stayed in Walnut Cove. John made iron products for the Confederacy; he would do so within the United States.

John and Julia followed the iron trade to several different towns and into Southwest Virginia. Julia bore John nine children, so many people today draw their life from the woman of action.

On cold winter nights when the family would gather around the fire, a child might have asked, "Oh, Mother, won't you tell us your war tale?" In most homes, it was the man that regaled the family with war accounts; but in the Moore house, the woman told the tales.

Courtesy: Gertie Hopper

Holy Smoke

The bells of Abingdon rang wildly that day in April 1861. Each church's bell had its own pitch, and they intermingled in a cacophony of excitement. War! War! War! echoed human voices in the streets. A day of fun and joy lay ahead, but the bell of Saint Thomas's Espiscopal Church tolled deep and somber under the high pitch of the others. It was almost like the rumbling of summer thunder, almost like a cannonade heard from afar.

The massive, iron bell had called worshippers together many times; but this time was special.

The first pipe organ west of the Blue Ridge had filled the sanctuary with music before, but this time was special. Prayers were said for the boys all across the South who were volunteering in droves, and special blessings were invoked on the youth of Saint Thomas who would go.

Old- Saint Thomas Church

The church was only fifteen years old. Most of the founding families were still in the pews. The Triggs, Prestons, Johnstons, and other families with common religious and blood lines gathered together on that spring day. The young men smiled and grinned eagerly, as they awaited the churchs' blessings before marching off to a hero's war. They would go with God, for the glory, and the adoration of the girls.

Young men and their belles beamed, but some of the older members were more somber. They recalled a similar service years ago. The church family blessed and bade farewell to John Preston Johnston. He never came home from the Mexican War. How many Johnnys would the pastor bless today, they wondered?

Saint Thomas Episcopal was not the first or only church to take its bell from the tower. There was discussion before the massive, iron bell was sent from the house of peace to war. The bell would not be silenced. By agreement, it was used to make Confederate cannons. Yankees would see righteous fire and Holy smoke from the Saint Thomas Church.

The boys from Saint Thomas and Washington County took their places in the Confederate ranks. A few county boys didn't believe in the Cause, and they marched north. From the area, Thomas Preston became a colonel. Robert Trigg led his 54th Virginia first to Kentucky and then joined Joseph E. Johnston's Army of the Tennessee. The 54th Virginia was unusual. Most of the boys who didn't fight in the area joined Lee or Stonewall, but the 54th Virginia followed their "Uncle Joe."

Those who prayed for the young warriors in the Spring of 1861 wept as news of the deaths and horrible wounds of county sons spread. In 1864, the church opened its doors, but the crowd was so big; it filled the sanctuary, church lot, and streets. The Department Commander, Gen. John Hunt Morgan, had fallen. The crowd of civilians and soldiers that followed his bier formed the largest funeral procession to ever occur in Southwest

Virginia.

High and mighty generals and lowly privates died, but their deaths could not keep the Confederate States of America alive. Saint Thomas's bell greeted the birth of the nation, but only silence could be given at its passing.

The Southern people truly thought they were creating a new Camelot of lords, ladies, chivalry, and honor. The South was in ashes; the Confederacy destroyed; but the dream remained alive in those who struggled for The Lost Cause.

Monuments and memorials were raised to the fallen Cause and to the dream world it represented. Mrs. Robert W. Hughes, with church permission, had two windows installed to honor those from the Saint Thomas Church in two wars. One window was to remember her brother Lt. John Preston Johnston who was in the War with Mexico. The other was to one of the South's greatest generals, Joseph E. Johnston. The windows were probably made by Tiffany and Company and installed shortly after the war. By 1924, it became evident that the windows must be repaired if they were to be saved. They were removed for reconditioning.

Two days after the church celebrated the birth of the Savior, at 11:30 P.M. a fire raced through the church. Only the altar cross, the processional cross, and the altar service book were saved. The pipe organ was lost, and all church records went up in smoke.

Many who worship believe that God is mindful of man: that God does work in and through men. The windows were removed before the fire and now form an integral part of the new church. The windows are preserved for this generation; was it by accident or incident?

Courtesy: Reverend Victor C. Mansfield
Saint Thomas Episcopal Church
124 East Main St.
Abingdon, Va. 24210

155
Eugenis Summers Phillips

Washington County Historical Society
Old Courthouse
Abingdon, Va. 24210

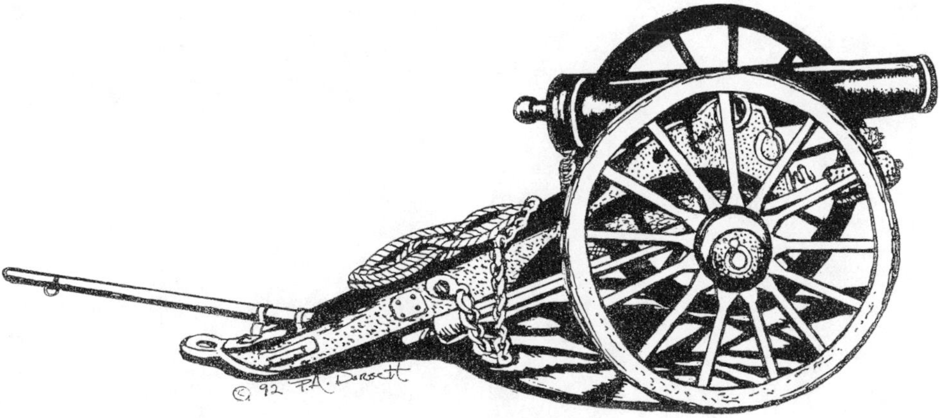

Dorsett Portraits
Patsy Arrington Dorsett
234 W. Augusta Ave.
Vinton, Va. 24179

HIS LIFE'S END."
AND IN MEMORY OF
JOSEPH E JOHNSTON
BRIGADIER GENERAL·U·S·A
GENERAL·C·S·A
BORN·FEBRUARY 3,1807
DIED·MARCH·21 1891

BLESSED·ARE·THE·PURE·IN·HEART.
FOR·THEY·SHALL·SEE·GOD."
AND IN MEMORY OF
JOHN PRESTON JOHNSTON
LIEUTENANT U·S·A
BORN·FEBRUARY 1,1824
FELL·IN·THE·SERVICE·OF·HIS·COUNTRY
AT CONTRERAS, MEXICO
AUGUST·19,1847.

BEHOLD THE MAN

Ever since the publication of my first book **The War in Southwest Virginia 1861-65** I have been in much demand as a speaker. I have spoken to many historical, educational, and civic organizations.

I received an invitation to address an association sponsored by a college; the group would be composed of local residents, as well as those on the staff. (All names have been deleted because I do not wish to embarrass anyone other than myself).

As often happens, the invitation to speak was coupled with an invitation to dine. The lady who invited me and her husband took me to a very elegant restaurant which was housed in a beautiful antebellum building. I did not feel a bit out of place as I took my seat dressed in my Confederate uniform.

Before the meal was served we , of course, engaged in some small talk. The subject we naturally had in common was the war. I was impressed with the knowledge of history that both of them had. It was clear from the conversation that the husband had read one of my books; I assumed she had also (That was my first mistake).

After some conversation had passed, she asked me how I would like to be introduced to the group. In a wink, my mind raced: phrases like "The world's greatest author...faster than a speeding locomotive ... able to leap tall buildings in a single bound," came to mind. So I said, "Whatever words you think will be appropriate will be fine with me."

Then I waxed philosophical (That was my second major mistake). "The greatest introduction I know of only had three words," I said. "When Jesus was brought before Pontius Pilate's court, the soldier simply said, 'Behold the man.' Maybe someday, I will be so well known that someone will introduce me with the same words," I said - tongue in cheek. I was joking, of course, that I would ever be as popular as Jesus Christ. I assumed she knew I was joking (That was my third mistake).

Later at the meeting hall, I sat up front with my head humbly bowed waiting for my introduction. Because my mouth often gets dry when I speak, I placed a breath mint in my mouth. The lady advanced to the rostrum to do the honors. I waited with eager ears to hear words of praise drip like honey from her mouth before I took center stage.

With a wave of the arm and a point in my direction, she said - "Behold the man!"

I now realized all the folly of my ways. A wave of great embarrassment, mixed with self-abasing humor, swept over me. I darned near swallowed my breath mint whole. It took me by so much surprise that I cannot recall to this day the first few sentences of that speech. I did recover, and the audience seemed to enjoy my talk.

I hope they learned a little about the war that day. I know I learned what not to say when someone asks me, "How do you wish to be introduced?"

Courtesy: Gary C. Walker

The Flag & Religion

He spoke in a soft voice with a Southern accent. Even his gestures indicated that this was a gentle man. As he spoke, the crowd about him stopped moving and became silent. His soft voice traveled, and all those about listened attentively because they just knew this man had something to say that they wished to hear. He spoke to all in earshot, but it seemed as if he were speaking to each individually.

Courtesy: Major Vass Hale Collection

"The flag is a religious symbol," he said, gesturing toward the Confederate battle flag. Everyone present was familiar with the red, white, and blue flag; that fought against the red, white, and blue flag; but no one present had ever thought of the flag in religious terms.

"The Confederate Congress wanted the flag to reflect the greatest principle of the new nation. It was no mistake or accident that they adopted this flag.

The flag features a cross on its side.

The cross of Christ was erect, as you know. Tradition has it that when Saint Peter was crucified that he requested his cross to be placed up side down because he did not believe that he was as good as Christ. So, Saint Peter's cross was up side down.

When Saint Andrew faced the same fate, it is said that he requested his cross to be placed on its side because he didn't feel as worthy as either Christ or Saint Peter.

By adopting this flag, the Congress was making the statement that the Confederate States of America were founded on Christian principles."

When he finished speaking, the crowd began to move and to make noise again. All present knew that they would view the Confederate flag in a new way when they left. They knew this gentle man had touched them deeply, but many didn't know his name. It was not uncommon to hear whispers in the crowd, "Who was he? Who was he?" Some people knew and replied, "John Hurley." "Who is John Hurley?" some asked. As the crowd went their way someone said, "He is a true Southern gentleman."

Courtesy: John Hurley
Confederate War Memorial Association
Confederate Memorial Hall
1322 Vermont Ave. N. W.
Washington, D. C. 20005

A STRANGE SONG

When we reflect on the military part of the war, in our mind's eye, we see soldiers entrenched about Petersburg; we visualize Federal troops battling mosquitoes, marshes, and the Confederate Army along some tributary of the Mississippi; we see troops force marching over the plains or cavalry troops stumbling over some mountain road in a midnight thunder storm; but the War Between the States was fought around the world.

Most visitors to the elegant hotel give little notice to the massive world map on the wall. Very few inspect the red lines on the chart. Because this was an English sea outpost, world maps are a very common sight. Only when the visitor takes time to read the legend does he realize that the red lines trace the course of the Confederate raider, **The Alabama.** Why would the **Alabama's** world voyages be recorded on this wall in a South African hotel?

The only language we associate with the war is English. A visitor from the States may hear school children singing this song in the streets of Cape Town and not associate it with our war.

Daar-kom die A-li-ba-ma, die A-li-ba-ma - die
Kom oor die see ----
Daar-kom die A-li-ba-ma, die A-li-ba-ma - die
Kom oor die see,
Noi, Noi, die riet-kooi, Noi, die riet-koo
is ge-maak - die riet-kooi is vir my ge-maak
Om daar-op te slaap ---
Om daar-op te slaap, die A-li-ba-ma, die A-li-ba-ma,
Die A-li-ba-ma kom oor die see ----
Die A-li-ba-ma kom oor die see.

The language is Afrikaan. South Africa is a multi-cultural country. The Bushmen and Hottentots were there when the first white men arrived from the Netherlands. Then the British turned the tip

The Alabama

of Africa into their colony. The Nguni (blacks) then invaded or migrated for economic reasons. There is a large population of Indian nationals, Chinese, and other Orientals living there. Almost every nationality on earth is represented in South Africa. The folk song probably had two writers because the first verse seems to have little to do with the second, but they sound good in the Afrikaan dialect.

The advent of the song was the appearance of the **Alabama** off Cape Town in July 1863. A Federal ship the **Sea Bride** was also at the Cape. It appears that the **Sea Bride** at first mistook the **Alabama** for an English ship. Both the British flag and the Confederate flag share the cross of Saint Andrew. It appears that the **Sea Bride** was unarmed or lightly armed. The **Alabama** pulled alongside and fired point blank on the **Sea Bride.** It was only a powder charge, and no projectiles tore through the **Sea Bride**; but the Union captain got the message very loud and clear. Too late, the **Sea Bride** attempted to escape. The **Sea Bride** surrendered to the **Alabama** and followed her captor into Table Bay. All businesses in Cape Town closed, and the city's population lined the shore to watch the ships.

Raphael Semmes, the captain of the **Alabama**, was the "Hero of the hour." In fact, "For years, the visit of the **Alabama** was talked of in every bar in Cape Town." Throngs of people from Cape Town visited the ship. The people who visited could not help but note the unusual Southern drawl of the officers, and the familiar British accent of the crew. The British Empire was officially neutral but was pro-Southern in temperment.

The **Alabama** was built in England and manned by a British crew. Once in Table Bay at Cape Town, the British man of war **H.M.S. Valorous** positioned herself between the **Alabama** and the open sea, just in case a United States' war vessel should try to interrupt the festivities.

The **Alabama** was resupplied and refueled (coal) and put to sea, but her visit was not forgotten and is still sung about. Dr. Peter Lipron, a former South African subject, was kind enough to translate the song into English. Some Afrikaan words can have more than one English counterpart, so the translation is loose, but the meaning comes through.

There comes the **Alabama**, the **Alabama** comes over the sea.
Sweetheart, sweetheart, the reed (or cane) bed, sweetheart
The reed bed is made, the reed bed is made for me to
Sleep on, to sleep on.
The **Alabama**, the **Alabama**, comes over the sea
The **Alabama** comes over the sea.

Courtesy: Dr. Peter Lipron
Formerly of South Africa
and Richlands, VA.

The Embassy of South Africa
3051 Massachusetts Ave. N. W.
Washington, D. C. 20008

THERE IS NO ARGUING WITH A FIRING SQUAD

Troy and William Spencer were not among the gay boys of 1861. They watched that Spring as the smiling, eager, young men marched off to a short, glorious war. They were better educated than most of their rural Grayson County counterparts. Perhaps they knew that war was more than pretty new uniforms, speeches, and parades. Perhaps they looked beyond the glitter and saw the mud, blood, and pain. They didn't enlist when excitement and idealism filled the air.

One year later, the shine was off the brass; and blood was on the bayonet. Grim, older men knew something of the price of a Union torn apart.

By April 1862, the romance was gone; those who volunteered knew what they were stepping into. Both Troy and William pledged their lives in defense of the Confederate States of America. Both joined Company C, 63rd Virginia Infantry. Starting on April 6, William Spencer had to salute his superior officer, 2nd Lt. Troy Spencer.

Troy Spencer

William Spencer

They drilled at Abingdon, and at first were assigned to Kentucky General Humphrey Marshell. When they left the Department of Southwest Virginia, they were placed under General Joseph Johnston who was the head of the Army of Tennessee.

The Spencer boys saw much death and many dreary marches in Virginia, Tennessee, Georgia, and Mississippi. William was promoted first to corporal and then to lieutenant. He no longer had to salute his superior brother. Soon after achieving equal rank, Yankee gunfire ripped his body open. Although the blood flowed, the wound was not mortal; and Lieutenant Spencer rejoined

Lieutenant Spencer in the ranks.

Since July of 1863, William Sherman had pushed his massive army east from Vicksburg, Mississippi. Joseph Johnston and the 63rd Virginia fought delaying actions against Sherman every step of the way.

Johnston knew he couldn't take Sherman's hordes on in open-field battle and win, so he conducted a campaign of attrition against Sherman. He attacked Sherman's weak points and supply trains. Johnston would not sacrifice his men in needless battles but conserved them to fight Sherman when his supply line was the longest.

The soldiers loved their general, and nicknamed him "Uncle Joe" for his compassion. Many a Southern lady's son bore the name "Joseph" in his honor. The compassion of Joseph reached down through the ranks to the Spencer brothers. They were granted permission to travel to Southwest Virginia to visit their ailing mother. They left the army in June 1864. When they returned in July, Lt. Troy H. Spencer was informed that he had deserted and was under arrest awaiting a firing squad. It is not known why William didn't face the same fate.

The brothers wanted to appeal to "Uncle Joe," but he was no longer there. The President Jefferson Davis had decided to replace him with John Hood from Texas.

Hood had been severely wounded in battle and was consuming large amounts of laudanum (dope) to keep going. His judgment seemed to be impaired. He wanted to show that the friendly, non-fighter Johnston was gone and that the fighting, tyrannical Hood must be pleased.

Brother William frantically communicated to Southwest Virginia. It is not known how long it took Brigadier Gen. William I. "Mudwall" Jackson to send a letter. The quality of the letter is so poor that only parts can now be read, but Jackson stated that the boys had not deserted.

Even this word from a brigadier general was not enough to make Hood postpone the execution.

Again, William communicated with Jackson. In a second letter, Jackson stated that the Lieutenants "did service in the Department of Southwest Virginia."

Confederate mail traveled more slowly than Confederate bullets. An innocent lieutenant Troy H. Spencer was killed by his own troops. One Spencer died; many Spencers cried, but Hood was satisfied.

The Sister

Most probably, it was William who helped to bury his brother in the red clay of Georgia not far from Atlanta. In a final "salute" to his lieutenant brother, William bore a piece of Troy's shattered skull back home. "...Gruesome tho it sounds, a sister was given a fragment of her brother's skull which she kept in a red silk handkerchief as long as she lived."

Courtesy: Anonymous

Slave Tag

ANOTHER -NO STORY

This story has similarities to the first story in the book because there is so little information related to the photo. The photo is of the remaining part of a "slave tag." A slave tag was not used so much for identification as it was proof that the taxes had been paid on the slave around whose neck the tag hung.

This tag came from South Carolina but was recovered near Richmond and is now part of the Jeff Watkins' collection. Why would a slave from South Carolina be in Richmond? There are two probable answers: because of the massive trench works and fortifications in the Richmond-Petersburg area, tremendous numbers of slaves were brought in to help with the work.

Another probable answer is that it came from a slave who served alongside his master during the time when Grant's troops circled the area like a noose around the head of the Confederate capital. These, of course, are not the only possibilities.

We know nothing of the slave or his owner, and this story doesn't focus on a single slave or master; but is about the institution of slavery.

Because none of us living has ever personally witnessed institutional slavery, we view it as a quaint and, perhaps, a cruel institution. We attempt to apply our life experiences and morals from the late- twentieth century as we view that particular institution. Most people view slavery as a social institution.

Slavery is first an economic institution, then an historical institution, and then a social institution. Slavery's origins are as old as mankind. There are references in "Genesis" in the **Bible.** Slavery knows no skin color. Men of every skin color, and of the same skin color, have been both masters and slaves during the centuries of man's history.

In America, Indians held both white and black people in slavery. In the northeast section, it was more common that white people held white people in a limited form of slavery (the bondsman).

Sea captains, mostly from the North, brought Negroes from Africa to the South. Almost all of the arriving blacks were slaves before they left Africa. They were held in bondage by stronger tribes and sold to the sea captains.

Most slave owners in the Southern part of the United States were white owners of blacks, but it was not unheard of for blacks to own blacks.

Most people in the United States accepted (or ignored) the economic and social relationships of slavery. Those people who wished to destroy the institution and were willing to take a militant stand to do so were called abolitionists. They were a small minority.

Northern abolitionists' views were based on what they saw, heard, and read. They only saw and heard from runawayslaves. These were slaves who could not or would not fit into the society into which they were born. There were those who ran away on moral or idealistic principles, but there were also those who ran away because they could not or would not follow their society's rules. Neither class was typical of the majority of slaves. Slavery was just a way of life, and it was their life to live (for both slave and master). All societies have those who can't or won't follow a "normal" way of life. Great artisans and political thinkers are among these, but so is the panhandler and the criminal.

Northern abolitionist thinking was also influenced by literature. The one book that seems to have had the most impact on the movement was **Uncle Tom's Cabin.** It is a fictitious account written by a person who had never witnessed slavery firsthand. Since 1863, when slavery became an official Union reason for continuation of the war, there has been much written in condemnation of the institution. Once the South was occupied, the conquerors made sure that every school's history book was critical of the institution and heaped shame upon the Southern society for having black slavery. (Almost no mention is made of the bondsman system or colonial period black slavery in the North.)

Abolitionists condemned slavery as a "moral wrong." This placed them on very shaky ground. Most people from colonial days until the war, and many to this day, believe that the great moral principles of our society are set forth in the **Bible.** The abolitionists could find no comfort in the scriptures for their cause. Nowhere in the **Bible** is slavery condemned, but quite the opposite. Some references admonish Christians to be good slaves for Christ.

The abolitionists adopted a "higher moral law," to justify their campaign. They never defined its basis or said what it was higher than, but one must assume they meant higher than the **Bible** and the United States Constitution (which also recognized slavery).

To argue that slavery was a wonderful and idealistic way of life would be ludicrous, but to argue that capitalism is wonderful and idealistic would be equally as ludicrous. It was just one institution in human history. All forms of human society (from tribal, feudal, socialist, dictatorship, or capitalism) generate both pleasure and pain for those people in them. Whether one is a manager, a worker, an artisan, investor, slave, free, or bond life is a mixture of pleasure and pain. No institution that humans have tried has generated only pleasure and no pain. Social institutions are not inherently "good or bad." A slave economy was no exception.

There have always been those people who, because of lack of judgment or for ego reasons, use their power to take excessive advantage of those under them; and slave owners were no exception.

Many people believe that slavery was such a savage and cruel institution that if given a chance, the slaves would rise up and murder their "evil" owners. John Brown went to his grave with that belief.

The War Between the States, or Civil War, or War for Southern Independence, shattered that theory. In many cases, the plantations were almost denuded of white men because they served with the army. A few women could not possibly contain a slave uprising, but no uprisings occurred. Many instances are recorded where slaves willingly risked their lives to protect their owners.

History is full of ironies. From 1863 to the end of the war, eradication of Southern slavery was one of the Union's stated goals. When the war ended, the only country in North America to have legalized slavery was the United States of America. The Emancipation Proclamation allowed slavery to legally remain in Delaware, Maryland, Kentucky, Missouri, West Virginia, and parts of

Virginia. Slaves in these areas remained in bondage until state elections were held in the fall.

Some people believe that it is imperative that they take a moral position (based on late 20th-Century precepts) and condemn slavery and the society in which the institution existed. There are some who would distort history and turn America's largest war into a race war. They would define slavery and the society in which it existed as barbarous, wicked, and cruel.

Those revisionist historians who climb upon a soap box and heap condemnation on bones rotting in the grave are a hundred and thirty years too late. Their moral passion distorts lessons that could be learned from history. Those who judge others should hold themselves accountable to their own standards. When they condemn the social "evil" of a past society, then they also condemn themselves for the "evils" of our presentday society because they are a part of it. When young men murder each other for the right to sell illegal drugs on a particular street corner, they are a part of the "evil." When men, women, and children lie down to sleep on a cold sidewalk in the drizzling rain (while revisionist historians snooze in a warm mansion), revisionists condemn themselves. Before a person passes judgment on others, he should be sure that his house is in order first.

Since the early 1600's, many of America's black slaves have said, "Praise God for slavery!" They believe that leaving Africa and the institution of slavery in America was a very small price to pay for the opportunity to become Christians. Without crossing the sea, many believe they would be today living in a tribal hut worshipping a pagan god.

Slavery is almost as old as mankind. It involved untold millions of people; it is a subject too broad to be covered in a few pages. Because legalized slavery does not exist in the world today, we consider that to be normal; but from an historical point, these are very abnormal times.

This article was not designed to be an all-inclusive treatise on slavery, only an attempt to allow the reader to think in broader terms about the institution.

Courtesy: Jeff Watkins

Floyd Garner

Gary C. Walker

Rev. David "Mickey" Derrow
New Hope Christian Church
4229 Welcome Valley Rd.
Roanoke, Va. 24014

* * * * * * * * * * * *

About the Author

Gary Chitwood Walker was born on May 24, 1946, in Wytheville. He is the sixth and last child of Carl and Mary Walker.

Gary attended Spiller Elementary School. It was here in the Seventh Grade that the war bug bit him. The study of Virginia History exposed him to America's greatest war and started a fire in him that time has not put out. He thrilled to learn about massive battles and campaigns around Richmond, and in the Shenandoah. He asked the teacher, "What happened around here?" (Meaning Wytheville.) The teacher stuttered and stammered that she knew something happened, but didn't know what. Twenty-five years later Gary answered that question for himself and the rest of the world when he wrote **The War in Southwest Virginia 1861-65.**

In high school Gary showed little aptitude for math, but a great inclination toward social studies. Gary's fascination for Civil War history was heightened when he studied United States History under Miss Lelia Huddle. He graduated from George Wythe High School in 1964.

Gary wanted to study history in college but explained that "It required three years of foreign language to graduate, and I knew I could never get through three years, so I studied Business Administration." Nearly all of his elective hours were in history or political science. The blending of the two academic yields, history and economics, gives Gary a unique ability to analyse economic, historical, and political events. Coupled with his understanding of human psychology and sociology, it allowed him to give a more comprehensive evaluation of historical events. Gary graduated with a Bachelor Degree in Science from Virginia Polytechnic Institute in 1968.

Shortly after graduation, Gary married his long time sweetheart, Sue Adams. She originates from Max Meadows. Together they have two fine sons, Christopher Ewell and Kevin Forrest.

After graduating, Gary continued his education

studying among other things creative writing and photography.

Gary's love of history led him to investigate his family's history. This was his first serious, independent, research. It resulted in **Walker, Ben to Carl.** Later he researched and wrote **Footprints,** a history of the Adams family. No attempt was made to do a mass production of the books, but they did allow him to sharpen his skills for his later endeavors.

One of the characters in **Footprints** was involved in a battle in Southwest Virginia. Gary was shocked to discover there was nothing reliable in print on the area. At that point in the seventies, he began researching the subject.

Gary had a wide variety of jobs after graduating college. He was a manager, a sales representative, and a truck driver. He worked in electronic communications, in insurance, in energy conservation, and in retail sales and service among other fields. With the great success of **The War in Southwest Virginia 1861-65**, Gary knew he had found his niche

The book propelled him from obscurity. From 1985 until the present, one can often find Gary dressed in a Confederate uniform, speaking to audiences, granting interviews to radio and television and newspapers, at Civil War re-enactments, and at craft festivals autographing his books.

Encouraged by the success of **The War in Southwest Virginia 1861-65,** and by requests from the public for more, Gary researched and wrote **Hunter's Fiery Raid through Virginia Valleys.** It is the only detailed and accurate account of Union General David Hunters savage assault on Confederate military forces and on the Southern civilian population. Hunter fought many major and minor battles from Winchester to Lynchburg, then through the Roanoke-Salem area and back into West Virginia. Hunter left pretty towns, colleges, and fine plantation homes ransacked or in smoldering ashes.

The success of **Hunter's Fiery Raid through Virginia Valleys** increased Gary's fame and recognition of him as a force in the study of the war. Continuing good reviews and public requests inspired Gary to produce **Civil War Tales.** He sincerely hopes the public will accept this work as well as they have his previous books.

Gary is very pleased that so many people have been informed and entertained by his books. He enjoys hearing from students from grade school through the doctoral program in college, who have used his books as a resource material for their projects. He is pleased that nonacademics have used his books to help in genealogy research, or led them to uncover relics buried since the war. Others have used his work to write scene plays, and to produce carvings and sculptures. The Virginia Defense Force has used material from Gary's books in making a recruitment film.

Gary has received numerous accolades and citations for his work. One of the latest is a listing in **Who's Who in America** the South and Southwest edition.

His books have propelled him into leadership roles with both the Sons of Confederate Veterans and the Civil War Round Table. He is also a member of many historic and preservation groups among others.

Gary served on the research and writing committee for the Wythe County Bicentennial Pageant Committee. A poem he wrote covered the back page of the play program. Dressed in a Colonial costume to represent the spirit of the county's namesake, George Wythe, he opened the play by reciting a portion of the poem. He also assisted in the mock Civil War battle scene that was part of the play.

Sustained by a loving family and backed by a beautiful wife with the patience of Job to help him work on the manuscripts, Gary is gratified that so many from such diverse backgrounds found his books to be so useful, entertaining, and informative.

The Author's Other Books

Gary Walker has written other books on America's greatest conflict.

THE WAR IN SOUTHWEST VIRGINIA 1861-65 is the only book ever written on that strategic Southern military Department. You'll ride with some of the Union's best troops under the generalship of the excellent Stoneman, the determined Crook, and the inept Burbridge as they try to stop the salt and lead flowing to General Lee!

You'll join the Dixie boys in the trenches and brave overwhelming odds. Generals Breckinridge, Jackson, and the "Devil" Morgan and their men (perhaps your ancestors) gave it their all as they tried to push the invaders back again and again!

Over one hundred sources were used. This book is detailed with 362 footnotes, 7 maps, and 85 photos and drawings. This handsome hand-numbered edition has a colorful, eye-catching dust cover.

HUNTER"S FIERY RAID THROUGH VIRGINIA VALLEYS took three years to write, and it is the only accurate, detailed account of Maj. Gen. David "Black Dave" Hunter's campaign to destroy the Confederacy. With Lee's army pinned against Ri chmond, the South's critical supply-line could be cut at Lynchburg. If the flow of lead and salt from the Military Department of Southwest Virginia were stopped - the Confederacy would be doomed!

The self-appointed avenger, the fanatical abolitionist, Hunter reaped punishment on the slave-holding state of Virginia. Towns were burned, looting and wanton destruction were commonplace. Battle raged though-out the Shenandoah, at Lynchburg, Salem, and in West Virginia.

To receive information on these books send self-addressed stamped envelope to: A & W Enterprise Box 8133 Roanoke, Va. 24014.